CORDOBA

CUARTA EDICION

Texts: MIGUEL SALCEDO HIERRO
Prologue by: D. RAFAEL CASTEJÓN Y MARTÍNEZ DE ARIZALA

Photographien: Oronoz
FISA
A. Mas
Salmer
J. Ciganovic
Catalá Roca
Arribas
A. G. del Ministerio de Información y Turismo
Beascoa
Kindel

EDITORIAL EVEREST

Apartado 339 - LEÓN (ESPAÑA)

BRIEF HISTORICAL BACKGROUND

The thousand year old city of Córdoba holds an important and eminent place in the world because of its historical events and illustrious sons. The English writer, Toynbee, proves this by including it among the twenty main cities of the world, ancient or modern, of ecumenical value.

It is austere and somewhat severe to the eye without the dazzling scenery typical of other capitals. This could be, as our Ortega y Gasset says, because Córdoba could be compared to a rose tree upside down, with the roots in the air and the flower hidden under the earth.

Over many thousands of years, it has been the cradle of culture, perhaps because of its geographical disposition. It lies on the bank of an enlivening river, the river Betis or, as it is called now, the river Guadalquivir and touches on two regions, one mountainous and the other flat and arable in Jaén. This feature has lent the city all kinds of natural opportunities.

Prehistorical finds go back to the Chellean age and remains appear on the hills on either side of the river but most especially on the southern hills, following the archeological strata uninterruptedly to historical times.

During the metal age, Córdoba becomes the departure point or wharf for shipping these metals to the great waterway, because the proximity of bronze, silver bearing lead and even iron deposits. During the long bronze age and at the beginning of the iron age, it is converted into the political capital of the great Southern region of Spain, where the cheiftains from all the regions and tribes held their assemblies and meetings, according to the records of the first historians and together with Gadir, now Cádiz, became the ruling city of the southern peninsular, standing out among the two hundred cities of the great Tartesian empire.

The first historical records are of the Carthaginian age when the Cordovans who accompanied Hannibal during his march against Rome are mentioned. The city of Córdoba is conquered by the Romans in the year 206 B. C. This could be called the great Iberian age and many are the archeological remains found of this era. Some thirty years after, Claudio Marcelo, praetor, has the city built following the style of Rome, with great monuments and ramparts because he has made it the capital of the Ulterior Spain. Córdoba becomes the principal town for the struggles against Julius Caesar by Viriatus, Sertorius and the Pompeii.

During the middle of the first thousand years before Christ, Greek schools were founded thus forming the basis and growth of the great culture to be found in Córdoba. The Romans declare the city as Patrician Colony and Agrippa is appointed Protector from whence begins the intermarriage between the Roman patrician families and the natives of Spain. The surname Séneca is a clear example of this interrelationship with the Celts.

During Rome's silver era, the Cordovan poets invade the cenacles of the eternal city. Lucano is sacrificed by Nero because of dramatic jealousy.

When, in the third century, Constantine brought the Empire to Christianism, it was the great Cordovan bishop, Osio, tormented in some previous Coucils, who becomes the evangelizing spirit, who advises and decides and who writes out the Creed, formula of the Christian faith, thence forth recited in prayer in the Catholic religion.

The patrons of the city, St. Acisclo and St. Victoria, are the martyrs of greatest fame and importance, standing out among the martyrs of the era of persecution.

The invasion of the Barbarians, whose passing was like a bloody avalanche, did not hit Córdoba so hard as to make the city lose its Roman influence, and in fact, it ramains so, now under the imperial protection of Bizancius up to the last Arian Visigoth king's Leovigildo, conquest of the city towards the end of the sixth century, Leovigildo invades the city on learning that his son, Recaredo, has been converted to Catholicism, and who has discovered in this highly civilized and romanized Andalusian region the ideal foundations for creating a new Spain and in Córdoba itself the safest refuge from the persecutions carried out during the previous regime.

In 711 the arabs find Córdoba, a beautiful city with numerous and magnificent monuments, a modern cathedral dedicated to St. Vincent and the best ramparts and precinct in the whole of Andalusia. The creation of monasteries and convents is magnificent. Rodrigo, the last of the Visigoth kings, later to die in the battle of the Guadalete was born in Córdoba, and also Pelayo, his cousin, fled from the capital, was to become the leader and symbol of the independence of the peninsular.

After half a century of being under the political yolk of the Arabic empire of Damascus, a member of the Omeya dynasty, Abd al-Rahman ben Moavia, escaped from the exterminating massacre of the Abu-l-Abbas descendants, on finding Córdoba, creates a kingdom which is to last nearly two and a half centuries, during which time his successors in legitimate line reign. One of these successors, Abd al-Rahman III proclaims himself Caliph and turns the city, already very developed, into the great Western capital and one of the most highly populated cities in the world during that era.

During the golden age of splendour in the tent century (the fourth hegira of the Moslems) Córdoba becomes the jewel of the world, as the Saxon Nun, Hroseitha, had foretold. It has half a million inhabitants and towards the end of the century, under the reign of Almanzor, reaches a million inhabitants. It gives birth to first class sages in all branches of knowledge. The Aljama Mosque, enlarged by al-Hakam II with an unbelievable magnificence and splendour, holds the artistic gems set in the palatial buildings of Medina Azahara, introducing a new architectonic and artistic style into the whole of the West, Arab as well as Christian empires, the influence of which is still to be found in this day and age.

5

Partial aerial view of Cordova, centered on its famous mosque. ▶

It is from this dazzling tenth century and even from the following, that the great Pleiad of illustrious figures offered to History by Córdoba from no matter what race or profession, has sprung. The school of San Eulogio produced a wave of Latin scholars which remained till the Reconquest, while Aben Masarra and Aben Házam among the philosophers, Aben Zeidún and Ben Suhaid among the poets, Abulcasis and Algafequi among the doctors, Azarquiel and Maslama among the astronomers, Aben Hayán and the Rasis among the historians, to quote some symbolic names, formed a pleiad of knowledge and wisdom among many other learned men, fomenters of the sciences and letters who constitute an unextinguishable splendour of the race.

Like the Jews, Most of these men are of Spanish origen, settled in the country over many centuries and forming a single thought as happens with the atistotelism of the Muslem Averroes and the Hebrew Maimónides, who expresses the influence of the media on its men and a Western way of thought which has nothing to do with Eastern influences.

Standing out in contrast in that great cultural age, explorers and conquerors penetrated into the depths of the African continent and were even the forerunners in the discovery of América. Córdoba became the centre of riches and trade which stretched to the farthest known countries of that era, the reason for this being the armies of artesans working precious metals, ivory, cloth and embroidery (one district alone, that of the cobblers, now the San Andrés district, has five thousand workers recorded on the census) and many other industrial arts, who settled in the city. All this explainsthe assertion of the French archeologist, Terrasse, that Córdoba is one of the cities of the world which has urban ruins in a perimetre of kilometres around it.

The arrival of the Almoravides and the Almohades during the eleventh and twelfth centuries, bring about the down fall of the Córdoba of the Caliphs, but in spite of this, its illustrious figures and its artesans keep the embers of the past glories burning.

When Córdoba is conquered by San Fernando in the year 1236, it is already a provincial city although it plays an important part in the internal struggles during the Early Middle Ages and above all it provides a valuable strategic point against the Moorish kingdom of Granada which is to survive two and a half more after the conquest of the Guadalquivir valley.

It is, in fact, the preparation for the conquest of Granada and the fact that the Catholic Kings make Córdoba their centre of operations, what returns some fleeting days of glory to the city where great men still burn bright in the heart of it, men like the Great Captain, descendant of the grand family, the Fernández de Córdoba, like the magnificent painter, Bartolomé Bermejo and a superb Cordovan school of painting (dynasty of the Fernández, Antonio Pérez, the master of Fuente Obejuna, Antonio Aguilar, Alejo Fernández, etc.) which, with sculptors and artesans, places Córdoba in an unrivalled position during the Renaissance period.

During the sixteenth century, Córdoba gives birth to poets like Juan de Mena and Juan Rufo, to historians like Ambrosio de Morales, Philip II's chronicler, like Juan Ginés de Sepúlveda had been shortly before to Charles V, to the great master of painting, Pablo de Céspedes, Prebendary of the cathedral and to many others. Cervantes'family, for many generations up to his grandfather and father, were worthy Cordovans and then later don Luis de Góngora, the poet, was to rise in fame, and don Angel de Saavedra, Duke of Rivas was born towards the end of the eighteenth century. Both of the latter two were revolutionaries in the world of literature. And during the last century saw the birth and rise of the excellent novelist and polygraph, Juan Valera.

This brief outline and background on important and famous symbolic figures bears out the assertion that Córdoba is the cradle of knoledge and sages and school of masters. The motto of the city «House of warriors and illustrious fountain of knowledge» has been crying out this truth over many centuries.

Special note should be taken of the Cordovan contribution to the great Spanish feat, the discovery and colonialisation of América, which was planned in this city which is full of reminiscences of Columbus. It was here that Cristopher Columbus obtained the aid of the Catholic Kings for his daring enterprise, while they were in Córdoba bent on the conquest of Granada. Adventurers and illustrious family names, names of towns (there are eighteen Cordobas in the American continent) missionaries and artesans, carried the Cordovan riches together with the flowing of blood and Spanish spirit, to fill and enrich the conquered land.

All along its history, Córdoba has produced spiritual and fine artistic works. There are even some historians who talk of a magic stick which touches men and families, making the anonymous into great figures, of the race fed on all beliefs and appearing in all the avatars of history.

It is said that the four great philosophers of the world are Cordovans. Séneca in the classic pagan world, Osio in the christian world, Averroes in the islamic world and Maimónides the Mosaic reformer of Hebraism. Blanco Belmonte, writer from the last generation, asserts in all the great feats of the world, a Cordovan names has some relation, whether in close connection or at a distance.

While the clear Cordovan horizons are glimpsed, while walking round its streets and marvelling at its monuments, while gazing at the perfumed patios full of flowers, while reading historical records or discovering archeological remains, the visitor should keep in mind that he is in one of the very few places in the world where the race scintillated under the purest divine commands of progress and culture.

RAFAEL CASTEJON
Director of the Royal Academy of Córdoba.

CORDOBA'S RAMPARTS

In ancient times, Córdoba was completely surrounded by ramparts and although modern buildings have grown beyond what was its mediaeval precinct, long stretches of ramparts have been preserved and stand witness to its ancient structure.

The precinct of Córdoba was divided into two large sections: the Almedina and the Ajerquía, both enclosed in independent fortifications and separated by a divided wall which can still be seen along the street of the «Feria» or of San Fernando. Narrow passages provided communication between the two fortifications and in the abovementioned street one can still cross one of these passages which is called «El Portillo» or the «Wicket».

The ramparts to the south are of extreme interest and the beauty and tranquility of its stone construction is reflected in the river Guadalquivir which flows by their side. From its towers —easily accessible— the visitor can gaze at the centuries old view of the famous Roman bridge, which in its time formed part of the great Vía Augusta and the old mills, the most outstanding of which is that called Albolafia, built against the rampart on the banks of the river like a sturdy support for the enormous wheel which collected water to irrigate the gardens of the fortress.

The ramparts disappear among the buildings in the quarter of the «Alcázar Viejo» but reappear at the beginning of the «Campo Santo de los Mártires» presenting a beautiful view of stone, vegetation and water in incredible architectonic harmony in the place called «Calle de la Muralla».

Most of the rampart's gates have been destroyed with the passing of the centuries and today names alone remain. The gate called «Puerta de Sevilla», however can still be seen with its two identical arches and which was originally built during the tenth century. Also still standing is the gate of «Almodóvar», framed with horse-shoe decorated arches and with two magnificent keeps on either side and the «Puerta del Puente» —built by Hernán Ruiz in 1571— which is completely Renaissance in style, with its fluted Doric columns and built on the site of an ancient Roman gate called by the Arabs the «Puerta de la Figura» because of the figure carved on its arch.

Arch of the Small Town Gate. ▶

The Albolafia mill, on the Guadalquivir.

The Seville Gate and monument to Aben Házam.

Walls and gardens at the Almodóvar Gate.

The Bridge Gate.

THE ROMAN BRIDGE AND THE CALAHORRA

The Roman bridge in Córdoba was built in the times of the Emperor Augustus, but over the twenty centuries since it was firts built, it has been the scene of so many battles and revolutions that only the ashlars and perhaps some of its arches remain of the original construction, since, mainly for military reasons they were alternatively destroyed and re-built.

The bridge was built on sixteen arches supported by buttresses which protect half cylindrical breakwaters decorated with half cones. The bridge has been reformed many times and during the first third of this century during one of these reforms, part of its Moslem stonework —outbond and inbond— which was perfectly identificable was covered with cement thus losing some of its singular archeological beauty.

In the year 1651, a statue of the Arcangel Raphael, work of the sculptor, Bernabé Gómez del Río, was placed in the middle of the bridge on one of its stone balustrades.

The last reformation was carried recently in the year 1965. An arcade was added next to the end of the left bank of the river Guadalquivir to counteract the force of the water next to the foundations of the fortress which rises against the abovementioned end of the bridge and which is called «La Calahorra».

The «Calahorra» is built in the shape of a cross and on the three arms rise three towers with battlements joined by bodies of the same height and built between the square towers. Its walls display the royal arms of Castille.

The building has been preserved just as it was originally in 1369 with only the very slightes modifications. It was built on the orders of King Henry II over a Muslem fortress, in order to reinforce the defence of the city which fought with him during the long struggle against his brother King Peter the Cruel, whose armies and the Moslem armies, his allies, were defeated by the Cordovans in the battle of the «Campo de la Verdad», which lies next to the fortress.

The city's Historical Museum is now installed in the rooms of the «Calahorra».

Image of San Rapha-el on the Roman bridge.

The bridge, the mosque and the Al-cázar of the Christian Kings in the 19th century, according to an en-graving by David Ro-berts.

Interior of La Calahorra, today seat of the Historical Museum of the City.

Oh sublime wall, oh towers crowned
with honor, majesty, and gracefulness!
Oh great river, great king of Andalusia,
of noble sands, even if not golden!

THE TOWER OF THE MALMUERTA

In the middle of the North-west corner of the Colón square, is an old octagonal tower, completely solid up to the height of the arch. For many years the city's rampart stood against this tower which is called «de la Malmuerta».

There is only one octagonal room inside the tower which is accessible from outside by narrow small windows decorated with small ashlars and crowned by a dome in the shape of a half orange. From this room a narrow passage leads the way to a second stair case which goes up to the high terreplein from where one has a very interesting view of Córdoba.

Under the arch, are stones with lettering confirming that the «Torre de la Malmuerta» was built between 1406 and 1408 on the orders of don Enrique III of Castilla, thus proving that the construction was carried out in the Christian era, but the beauty and delicacy of the battlements and the bows carved round the place where they are supported reveal the exquisite beauty of the Arab decoration typical of the style used by the Arabs settled in Spain. But taking into account that it was the Moors who were used for labour in the construction of the beautiful tower, it is not strange that this style should predominate.

The legend of the tower and the name given is that a noble, anscestor of the Marquises de Villaseca, killed his wife believing her to be guilty of adultery although this had not been proved, and on realising that he had committed an injustice, he repented this act and begged forgiveness of the king who condemned him to the building of this expiatory tower in remembrance of noble lady who died innocent of the crime she was accused of.

Popular tradition relates the legend of the tower with the historical fact of «Knight Commanders». Fernan Alfonso, known as the Veinticuatro de Córdoba, brutally revenged his honour offended by his adulterous wife by killing her and two relatives, the Knight Commander of Cabeza del Buey and the Knight Commander of the Moral, both Knights of the Order of Calatrava.

The town's verses deformed the facts, but presented no obstacle for Antón de Montoro who used the argument in some octaves of major poetical value. However, it was an anonymous song composed shortly after the tragedy which spread the news far and wide. The Juror of Córdoba, Juan Rufo, related the event in a long romance and finally Lope de Vega wrote his great tragedy «Los Comendadores de Córdoba» based on the poem by Juan Rufo.

All this magnificent historical, legendary and poetical contribution is coupled with the «Torre de la Malmuerta» for ever.

Malmuerta tower. ▶

THE FORTRESS OF THE CHRISTIAN KINGS

On the orders of king Alfonso XI, the Just, the building of the «Fortress of the Christian Kings» was begun in 1328, and was to be the royal residence. The fortress was enlarged during the dinasty of the Trastamaras with importants works such as the gardens, fountains, ponds and baths. Later, the Catholic Kings carried out reforms to make it habitable for them during the last military operations which were to lead to the conquest of Granada.

The last Moorish king of Granada, Boabdil, was kept prisoner in this fortress which received Cristopher Columbus for an audience with the Christian Monarchs before embarking on the journey which would lead to the Discovery of América. It was in this stronghold that the Inquisition was established from 1490 to 1821; later it became the provincial prison to be rescued in 1951 and returned to the city. It was given back its beauty as a mediaeval palace with delicate restoration works.

It was built in the form of a square fortified enclosure with a tower on each corner. The face of its walls are irregular stone ashlars placed outbond and two inbond, ending in walks for the guards with battlements and small narrow windows which provided communication between the towers with stairs for the different levels.

One of the above-mentioned towers, the one called the «Vela» (the «Candle») was destroyed in the nineteenth century. The other two, however, still stand; one called the Tower of the River, cylindrical in shape and with three floors comprising a first more ancient body with small narrow windows in the shape of a cross and a second body bricked in the shape of a prism on top of which is the third and highest body. The other, called the Tower of Homage is octagonal in shape with a large domed room or hall. The dome is ribbed with beautiful Gothic capitals and interior narrow slanting windows. Lastly, there is the Tower of the Lions which is the most ancient and most interested of the three, with its Gothic style dome formed by the crossing of the arches which rise from the capitals decorated with ferns. The exterior of the tower is worked in the style of the Arabs who settled in Spain typical of the era from the 13th century to the 16th century. Below this tower is the present entrance to the fortress.

Inside the building, the galleries are low-roofed with brick domes which lead the way to the large royal hall and among the many valuable archeological samples to be admired, is a marble tomb, a masterful work of funeral art during the second and third century and seven very valuable Roman mosaics of which the one of «Psiquis and Venus» with the four seasons of the year and the one of «Polifemo and Galatea» are worthy of special attention.

The ancient baths worked by steam should be visited. They are very well preserved as well as the beautiful Arab style patio. A walk through the gardens is to be specially recommended with its magnificent landscaping of trees, flowers, pools and illuminations. Artistic festivals and other public acts of the city are often held in these gardens

Alcázar garden walls.

Moorish patio in the Alcázar.

The tower of Lions, in the Alcázar.

Roman sarcophagus in the Alcázar.

Roman mosaic representing Polyphemus and Galatea, conserved in the Alcázar.

Magistral González Francés Street borders the northern side of the mosque.

The Almodóvar gate and the monument to Séneca. ▶

A beautiful view of the gardens of the Alcázar.

◀ La Calahorra and the back of the mosque.

Another view of the gardens of the Alcázar.

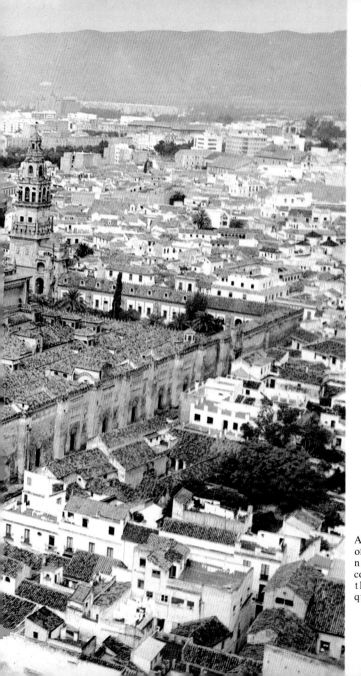

Aerial view of the magnificent complex of the mosque-cathedral.

San Esteban Gate, the most primitive in the mosque.

THE MOSQUE IN CORDOBA

Córdoba's mosque is the most portentous monument of Moslem Spain. That precisely it was built in the city worthy of the title given it of the first capital in the Western world and the interest and effort put into its magnificent construction by the caliphs as well as by the architects and artists working on it, justify the exceptional importance of this singular building, its later changes and the growth of its value with the passing of time. After the Mosque of Caaba, this one was the largest in the world and represents the zenith of the era of splendour during the reign of the caliphs in Córdoba.

The Mosque in Córdoba is now a mixture of superimposed architectonic styles over the nine centuries during which the building and reformations were carried out. It would seem that no generation passed without leaving its mark on this unique edifice, unique in its physiognomy and originality of its whole.

Like all mosques, the one in Córdoba has a patio in front, with fountains which were formerly used for the ritual ablutions, large naves dedicated for prayer and its «qibla» or wall in front of the entrance in the centre of which is a small chapel or niche called «mihrab» which was used to determine the direction to be faced when the Moslem was at prayer.

The mosque in Córdoba was a «Aljama» mosque because it had a «minbar» or pulpit where the preacher or «jatib» gave his sermon, called by the Arabs «Jutba» in which it was indispensable to name the reigning caliph.

The building of the mosque was started towards the end of the 8th century —year 785— under the rule of Abd al-Rahman I. It was built over the site of the Visigothic cathedral of St. Vincent, changing the bearings of the axis of the site. It had eleven aisles going from north to south and the central nave being much wider than the others.

During the year 833, Abd al-Rahman II enlarged the mosque to the south and built on a new «mihrab». The richest part was added by the caliph al-Hakam II in 961 and later on the cheiftain, Almanzor, completed the work giving it its present proportions.

In 1236, the Mosque was converted into cathedral by St. Fernando and chapels, decorative and other attributes and symbols of the Catholic religion where then constantly being added to it. The centre part of the mosque was destroyed in the 16 th century so that a choir, high altar and transept, main characteristics of all christian cathedrals, could be built in its place.

THE EXTERIOR OF THE MOSQUE

The site of the mosque is rectangular in shape and from North to South measures 180 metres and from East to West, 130 metres, thus making the total area 23,400 square metres. Within this area is the mosque itself and the «Patio de los Naranjos», «The Orange Tree Patio». Around it on the outside, runs a rampart topped with battlement cresting and fortified with square keeps among which are the several entrances to the building.

On the north side is the main door to the temple which is called today the «Door of Forgiveness» and was built in 1377 in the superb style of the Arabs. On this side there is also another door built in the Graeco-Roman style which·is called the door of the «Great Pipe» and beside it is a retable with wrought iron where the «Virgen of the Lanterns» is worshipped. It is an excellent copy of the picture by the Cordovan painter Julio Romero de Torres. From this side the Tower can be admired. It is the work of Hernán Ruiz, built over the remains of the Arab minaret raised by Abd al-Rahman III and topped with a «St. Raphael» sculptured by the Cordovan Pedro de Paz.

In the Western wall are the following doors: The «Postern Milk Door» with a Gothic pointed arch, and so called because the foundlings were left there in olden times to be sheltered by the clergy there and the «Deans Door», built in the time of Abd al-Rahman II. The last two doors lead to the «Orange tree Patio». Following this and corresponding to the interior of the mosque is the beautiful «St. Steven's Door» with straight hollow, horse shoe arch and a radial design of voussoirs alternating with groups of red bricks well fitted in: then St. Michael's Door, reformed in the 16th century with Gothic pointed decoration; the three doors towards the end of the wall, the centre one of which, called the «Palace or Dove Postern» requires special attention to its beautiful Gothic ornamentation dating back to the end of the 15th century. Finally, one can see a small door which leads to the passage which joined the mosque to the Caliphs' fortress over small bows.

The South face displays some thick buttresses fortified with towers. Towards the centre of the stretch of wall, the buttresses are thickened in order to compensate the influence of the arches inside the Cardenal's Chapel. Between the buttresses are some round arches with balconies which were built in the time of the Catholic Kings.

The whole of the Eastern face was added on when Almanzor enlarged the mosque. He had the style of the doors and arches copied from those built before in the time of al-Hakam II. There are two notable doors on this façade and they both give on to the «Orange Tree Patio». There is «St. Catherine's Door», elegant in the extreme and very markedly Renaissance in style, while the other, not named, is decorated in a very complicated and rather loud style.

34

Mosque. The Gate of Pardon, with Mudejar decoration from the 14th ▶ century.

Mosque. Gates and abutments on the eastern façade. ▶

Mosque. Detail of the Gate of Pardon.

THE ORANGE TREE PATIO AND THE ORIGINAL MOSQUE
OF ABD AL-RAHMAN I

On entering the precinct of the mosque by the «Door of Forgiveness», one immediately feels overpowered by the vision of the «Orange Tree Patio» with its green rows of trees from which it has taken its name, and which in spring are in full splendour with the flowering of the orange blossom. Upright cypruses make a happy interruption in the rows of orange trees, while graceful, swaying palms lend lively touch giving the whole a splendour framed by the stone ashlars and surrounding arches.

The stone Baroque fountain with its four spouts is very interesting. A well dating back to the 10th century during the reformation carried out by Almanzor, is also noteworthy.

Speaking in all historical strictness, this was originally the patio where the ablutions were doneaccording to customs in that time. Now it is somewhat changed due to the modifications suffered over the centuries.

In the height of its splendour, after the enlargement carried out by Almanzor, the Mosque had nineteen horse-shoe arches which lead directly from the patio to the hall of prayer. Today, nearly all of them are closed because they now give on to the back of the christian chapels which surround the inner precinct.

In front of the tower, the straight symmetry of a stoned street leads one to the «Door of the Palms», also known as the «Arch of Blessings» because it was before this arch that the armies banners and flags were blessed before leaving to conquer Granada.

The Arab stone built into the façade is very interesting because it refers to the walls' consolidation at this place and the two large Roman columns originally from the «Vía Augusta», discovered in the 16th century in the centre of the Mosque when excavating to lay the foundations for the transept.

One enters the mosque by «Door of the Palms» which leads to the original building. This was built in 785 on the command of the Emir Abd al-Rahman I in order to be able to attend to the inevitable growth in the Moslam religion. One can easily see that the original mosque had eleven naves from North to South and twelve spans of arcade running from East to West, because the later additions to the mosque are clearly defined. The central nave is wider than the others and coincides exactly with the «Door of the Palms».

Mosque. Gate of the Palms. ▶

Mosque. Fountain in the Patio of the Orange trees.

Mosque. Eastern gallery of the Patio of the Orange trees, where the Arab judge administered justice.

ABD AL-RAHMAN I'S MOSQUE AND ITS ADDITIONS

The eleven original naves in the mosque built by Abd al-Rahman I are supported by pillars resting on pedestals which are buried under the present day paving because of their great depth. These pillars are placed in an order possibly relating to the colour of the marble shafts while the most beautiful are placed in the central nave.

The capitals, which belong to previous works, show an extraordinary variety: Ionic style, Corinthian and composite styles. Nearly all of them are Roman or Byzantine due to the fact that they were originally taken from the Christian basilica of St. Vincent which lay there before and on the site of which the Mosque was built.

The roofs were flat with wood panelling very well carved and painted in several coulours. The floors must have been of red brick which they would have covered with mats although this does not mean that in some parts it was not paved with marble.

The joining of pillars to each other, usually solved in many oriental mosques of that time by wooden or iron stays, was substituted in the Mosque for arches supporting nothing, in the air, intercalated between the pillars. They are horse-shoe arches made up of keystones and above these are groups of three red bricks alternating with voussoirs which complete the originality of the arches. The arches above the pillars are rounded and are indentical to the lower ones.

Past the first twelve spans of the arcade, one enters the first addition to the original Mosque. This was built on the command of Abd al-Rahman II and was started in 833. The eleven naves were prolonged to the south by eight spans. The «qibla» wall was perforated and the «mihrab» was destroyed to permit this work to be carried out.

This second building brings in a new style by ommitting the pedestals while contributing magnificent capitals which although most of them were originally from previous buildings, at least eleven of them were expressly carved by Cordovan artesans. The modillions are gradually reduced in size until they become simple projections. Of the pillar shafts, there are very notable ones to the back where the «mihrab» of this addition should have been.

The parts added by Abd al-Rahman II were those most affected by the destruction caused in the 16th when the choir, high altar and transept of the Christian cathedral were built on.

Mosque. Visigoth pedistal and naves of the mosque of Abd al-Rahman I. ▶

Mosque. Capital from the extension of Abd al-Rahman II.

Mosque. Naves of the extension of Abd al-Rahman II. ▶

◀ Another view of the primitive mosque, «wrought in blocks of silence and beauty».

Mosque. Entrance Arch of the extension of al-Hakam II.

Mosque. Restored gate of al-Hakam II, in the western façade. (detail). ▶

Mosque. View of the western façade and beginning of the southern.

Mosque. Naves from Abd al-Rahman I.

Mosque. Detail of an alabaster column in the extension of Abd al-Rahman II. ▶

Mosque. Naves of al-Hakam II.

Mosque. Two other views of the extension made by al-Hakam II.

The ostentatious chapel of the Lucernario or of Villaviciosa.

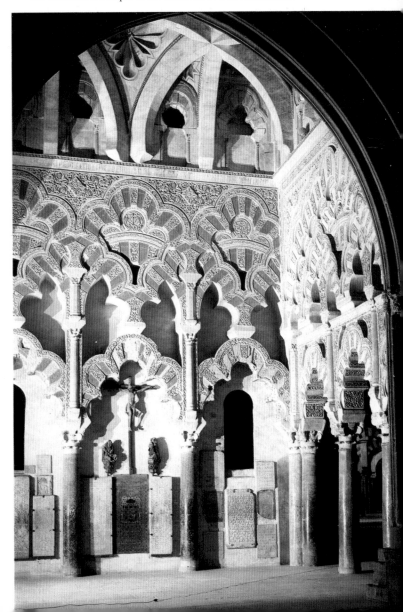

Detail of the dome in the vestibule cobba in the mihrab.

◀ Series of arches in the chapel of the Lucernario.

Mosque. Façade of the mihrab.

◀ Detail of the entrance arch of the mihrab.

Details of the skewbacks, capitals and shafts of columns of the entrance arch of the mihrab.

ADDITIONS MADE BY AL-HAKAM II. THE MIHRAB

The growing population in the city of Córdoba made enlargement of the Mosque necessary and the Caliph al-Hakam II gave the orders for additions to be built in the year 961. The eleven original naves were once more prolonged to the South and were criss-crossed with twelve spans of arcade definitely closed with the «qibla» and the new «mihrab».

These additions are the most beautiful of all. The pillars of these naves are alternated following a rhythm of colour, with no ornate bases and the capitals are of the composite or fifth order over rose coloured marble shafts and capitals of the Corinthian order over blue marble shafts. The roofing is of carved and multi-coloured panels.

Of the three existing pavilions at the entrance added by al-Hakam II, the centre one, now called the Villaviciosa Chapel is the most important, because there the art in the times of the Caliphs is desplayed in all its splendour. Its magnificent dome of hefty stone arches or ribs which give place to small domes all of which constitute a truly exquisite central work of art. This remarkably original dome was a contribution of Cordovan culture in the 10th century to world architectonic art. The engrailed and foliated arches bordering this remarkable precinct are also of extraordinary beauty with their intricate stone decoration as well as with their notable criss-crossing.

The eastern pavilion which is an exquisite example of Arab art in Spain, was reformed in the XIV century by King Henry II in order to make it into the «Royal Chapel» and the western one, the ornamentation of which was destroyed when the original Christian High Chapel was built in the XV century, is also very noteworthy.

The «mihrab» is in the central precinct of the three portieres which lead the way to the «qibla». The dome of this precinct or hall has a formidable octangular shape with double columns in the angles which support the eight crossed arches which make up the dome. It is decorated with a fascinating multi-coloured mosaic.

The façade of the «mihrab» rests on a marble panelled plinth. These panels are exquisitely carved. The horse-arch at the entrance covers nearly all of the front of the «mihrab» and is supported by two magnificent pillars —taken from the original «mihrab» built by Abd al-Rahman II— the voussoirs of which are covered in Byzantine mosaic. The spandrels of the arch are beautifully ornamented.

The moulding on the panel which covers the netting of the arch is double and over this panel rise seven foliated arches supported by very slender pillars thrown into relief by the interior ones of mosaic Moorish plaster work over a gold background.

The interior of the «mihrab» is octangular is shape and small. The original paving in this small room is still conserved and the dome is made up of one stone shell in one piece.

Dome of the chapel of the Lucernario or Villaviciosa.

Series of archs of the section preceding the mihrab.

General view of the dome of the section preceding the mihrab.

Series of archs of the interior of the mihrab.

ENLARGEMENT MADE BY ALMANZOR

The last phase in the construction of the Mosque was carried out in 987 during the reign of the caliph Hisham II on the decision of his Prime Minister, Almanzor. These additions are the largest and makes up nearly a third of the whole of the Mosque.

These last additions were built on to the East because of the situation of the River Guadalquivir which was already very close to the «qibla» built on by al-Hakam II. It ends at one of the two longitudes of its rectangular site, the east side of the parts of the Mosque built on previously. The «Orange Tree Patio» was also extended in proportion to these additions.

The material used for these additions built on the roders of this minister and Moslem chieftain, are less exotic and the building is more uniform than the previous ones. It comprises eight aisles and does not have the same importance as the previous additions since this epoch corresponded to the decadence of the Age of the Caliphs. It can be seen at first sight, that the pillars were not built with the same elegance as in previous additions and the capitals, although in the same style as those built by al-Hakam II, are somewhat narrower. Even the walls themselves are not so thick and the ornamentation on the outer portals —all on the eastern façade of the Mosque— is thrown instead of sculptured on the voussoirs as with the previous additions. All the arches built on, both the lower and the higher, are horse-shoe type and made of decorated and painted stone.

Before Almanzor's building was carried out, the edifice had, as was normal, a thick wall running along the eastern side. Therefore, wide arcades were built to provide communication with the new building. Some of these arcades are still intact and can be seen in their entirety.

Some of the pillars are of violet coloured marble and others blue and like the previously built ones are without plinths and instead of resting against isolated supports they rest on subterranean walls. The capitals are of the Corinthian and composite order.

With these additions ordered by Almanzor came the end of the enlargements of the Mosque. The only work carried out from then onwards was the work of conservation and the Mosque remained unchanged until Córdoba was incorporated into the kingdom of Castilla and León in 1236 by Fernando III, the Saint.

Entrance to the ancient passage way to the Alcázar of the Caliphs, to the right of the mihrab.

Expansion naves of Almanzor.

THE HIGH CHAPEL

The Córdoba Mosque was consacrated a Christian cathedral by the Bishop of Osma in 1236 under the appellation of the Assumption of the Holy Virgen. From then onwards, all succeeding bishops were tenacious in their attempts to carry out reforms on the exceptional Moslem work of art in order to make it more fitting for the Christian doctrine. During the xv century, the Catholic Kings allowed them to build a «High Chapel», next to the Villaviciosa chapel where the three longidutinal aisles were. The interesting wooden Gothic dome, full of Norman influence, is still preserved. During the xvi century, a new ecclesiastical pressure managed to overcome the strong opposition of the Municipal Council and the Cordavans who had to submit under the supreme mandate of Carlos I and were obliged to carry out the great reform in 1523, which, almost completely destroying Abd al-Rahman II's work and part of Alman-zor's, cutting through the centre of the marvellous architecture of the Caliphs to constitute the catholic temple. This reform, which finished in 1766 and lasted 243 years, contains a mixture of styles. The architect, Hernán Ruiz, began the work with pure Gothic characteristics, which then develops with a very marked herrerian influence ending in the pre-dominance of Baroque art.

The site of the «High Chapel» has the shape of a Latin cross. The arches are Gothic and the walls are low and decorated in Gothic style. The high walls, domes and windows are plateresque. The domes above the aisles and the transept are very similar to the roofs and domes in The Escorial.

The main altar piece was done in 1618 by the Jesuit, Alonso Marías, using jasper and marble from Carcabuey. It has five canvases by the Cordovan painter Antonio Palomino, which represent the Virgen of the Assumption in the centre and Acisclo, Victoria, Pelagio and Flora, saints and Cordovan martyrs. There are also figures of the Eternal Father, the Virtues, St. Peter and St. Paul, sculptured by Pedro de Paz in gold wood.

The Baroque tabernacle made of rich marbles, was finished in 1653 under the direction of the Master Sebastián Vidal and embellished with small figures sculptured by Pedro Freire de Guevara. The two mahogany pulpits, attributed to the Frenchman Miguel Verdiguier are an authentic example of Baroque art. There are some very interesting figures on the sounding boards and magnificent medallions on its frame as well as re-productions of Old Testament scenes. The pulpit on the side of the Epistle is supported by a white stone angel outlined over a lion of red jasper which is lying on a white marble cloud. The pulpit by the Gospel rests on the figure of an eagle of black marble and an enormous rose-coloured jasper bull which is almost life-size.

In the centre of the transept, can be seen the very impressive silver lamp, the work of the Cordovan silversmith, Martín Sánchez de la Cruz. The carved mahogany choir-stalls made in the XVIII by the Duke Cornejo are notable example of Baroque art. They are decorated with statues, reliefs and medallions and the episcopal throne stands out among them all. The lectern in the middle is well worth special attention. Above it is a niche with the ivory figure of the Holy Virgen, which is the original work of Alonso Cano.

◀ Another aspect of the expansion made by Almanzor, in which the space behind the altar can be seen.

THE CHAPELS IN THE CATHEDRAL. THE TREASURY

Over fifty chapels rest against the walls surrounding the Mosque. Their contribution to the fine arts is of great worth, because they represent the evolution of art in Córdoba through the centuries. Examples from every moment of the history of art can be found in the wrought iron work, the tile work, paintings and the sculpture there. Worthy of a special visit are: the «Conception» with work by the sculptor Pedro de Mena; the «St. Bartholomew» where the Cordovan poet, don Luis de Góngora y Argote is buried; the figure of «Cardenal Salazar», from the beginning of the XVIII century, which is the sacristy and the Chapter Hall, where among other valuable figures and paintings, stands the figure of St. Teresa, work of the sculptor from Granada, José de Mora; the «Incarnation», with a splendid panel by Pedro de Córdoba and a beautiful example of Arab art in Spain; the «St. Anne», with the altar piece painted by Pablo de Céspedes; «The Holy Souls» where Inca Garcilaso de la Vega is buried and the figure of «Our Lady of the Rosary» with magnificent paintings by Antonio del Castillo.

The Tabernacle, worked by Enrique de Arfe and used for the first time in the Corpus Christi procession in 1518, is held in the Treasury of Córdoba Cathedral. It is a singularly valuable piece of work. This gem of extraordinary worth is 2.63 m. high and weighs over 200 kilos. It represents a Gothic cathedral of dodecagonal shape and is made up of two bodies, one for housing the monstrance and the other for the image of the Virgen of the Assumption.

When the Tabernacle was restored in 1735, a base and other Baroque adornments were added to the steeples, buttresses and Gothic towers and lately in 1966, the monstrance has been given an aureole of diamonds.

The treasury also holds an excellent collection of pyxes and reliquaries, chalices and gold and silver ciboria, but the most important among the latter is the one attributed to Benvenuto Cellini.

Among the marvellous ivory crucifexes in the Cathedral treasury, the most noteworth is one carved in the XVII century by Alonso Cano and provides a magnificent study of the anatomy.

The four large crosses are worthy of special attention. Two are of gilt silver, one of rock-quartz set in silver —this is a magnificent example from the XVI century— and the other is of gilt silver with enamels, gold and previous stones. This latter cross weighs 80 kilos and was donated to the Cathedral by the Bishop Fray Diego de Mardones in 1620.

Detail of the Royal Chapel, Mudejar work of the 14th century.

OTHER ARABIC BUILDINGS

The Fortress of the Caliphs. The Mussulman governors adopted the palace of the Visigoth governors as their residence when they settled in Córdoba in 716. The basic part of this building still stands because the present episcopal palace was built over it, although the varied and substantial reforms carried out over the centuries have not left appreciable elements of the Arab domination except on the outside, where the original ramparts still stand on the side which faces the west face of the Mosque and on the North, joining the neighbouring building at an angle and down its common wall.

When the court of Abd al-Rahman III moved to Madinat al-Zahra, the outhouses, stables, baths, orchards and gardens of the Caliph's Fortress faded out into second place, but, however, they were once more put into full use with the Taifa Kings who took over the fortress as their residence. This was so, until 1236, when San Fernando donated the Fortress to the bishopric, after the city was reconquered

The palace holds a very interesting collection of portraits of the Bishops of Córdoba; several canvases and panels moved there from the churches in the diocese; a magnificent set of tapestries, among which stand out those donated by the bishop don Leopoldo de Austria together with his large and varied library to which was added the library from the Jesuit convent in the XVIII century.

The minaret of St. John and St. Clare. Among the remains of Arab buildings which still stand in the city, the minaret of the Mosque which the king granted to the knights of the Order of St. John of Jerusalem for them to establish their church, which is today the church of the convent of the Slaves of the Sacred Heart. The «Minaret of St. John» is a small tower, 8 metres high by 3.5 at its base, built with inbond and outbond stones. On each of its fronts is a window with double twin horse-shoe arches resting on a slim pillar as a mullion. The Conrinthian capital on one of them proves that the minaret was built in the time of Abd al-Rahman II.

There are also some remains of another mosque dating back to the time of Almanzor, in the Convent of St. Clare, of a Franciscan order. They consist mainly of tower faces and the arch at the entrance.

Arab baths. Only one of the many Mussulman baths in Córdoba still stands. It is in the street «Comedias» facing the entrance to the «Alley of the Flowers». It is still in good condition and has a hall with pillars, capitals and arches and a gallery surrounding it and a perforated dome which allowed the corresponding vents to work. There are also the remains of other Arab baths in one of the houses in the old «Fish market».

◀ Cathedral nave seen from the main chapel.

Exterior of the Episcopal Palace, ancient Alcázar of the Caliphas.

Episcopal Palace. Garden staircase (18th C.).

◀ Minaret of
the church
of San Juan

Marble
block with
ornamen-
ted plaster
work, in the
socle of the
front of the
mihrab.

The venerable dome of the mihrab.

Cathedral. *The Holy Supper*, canvas by Pablo de Céspedes.

Cathedral. Detail of the choir-stalls, work of Pedro Duque Cornejo. ▶

Cathedral. Canvas by Antonio del Castillo, in the chapel *of San Pelagio*.

Cathedral. *Annunciación*. by Pedro de Córdoba (1475).

Interior of the Synogogue.

THE SYNAGOGUE

Halfway down the street of the «Jews» is the Synagogue, the Hebrew temple. From the outside, one can barely guess that it is there for the reason that there is no direct entrance from the street, first one has go through a narrow yard.

The plane of the Synagogue is square. The wall which runs along the patio at the entrance is decorated, like the rest of the building, with plaster worked in the style of the Arabs, and over it is a gallery on to which open three small balconies for the women. On these balconies are some beautiful engrailed arches outlined with a panel with the inscription of the Psalms.

There is another inscription above the entrance, which could be translated thus:

BLESSED BE HE WHO HEARS ME AND FROM DAY TO DAY LEARNS FROM MY DOORS TO GUARD MY THRESHOLDS. OPEN THE DOORS AND LET THE NATION OF THE JUST AND FAITHFUL IN.

In the right hand wall is a hollow for the tabernacle where the Pentateuch rolls were kept and where lamps were kept incessantly alight. This easter wall is decorated with plaster where there is a central panel crowned with elegant arches, under which appears the word «blessing» in Cufic characters.

Along the whole of the frame of the tabernacle is a large Hebrew inscription with the words of a Psalm and in a rectangle, halfway up is another very interesting inscription. Its interest lies in the fact that it refers to construction of the Synagogue:

SMALL SANCTUARY AND REFUGE OF THE CONFIRMATION OF THE LAW FINISHED TO PERFECTION BY ISAAC MEJEB, SON OF THE GREAT EFRAIN, WAS BUILT, BORN OF A CERTAIN HOUR IN THE YEAR SEVENTY FIVE. OH GOD! ARISE AND BRING ON TIME WHEN JERUSALEM CAN BE REBUILT.

The year referred to is 5075, which corresponds to the Christian year of 1315.

The North wall which faces the entrance, is also covered with Moorish plaster work. The western wall has a pointed arch decorated with delicate foils which rests on a crenelated bracket holding the inscription in Cufic characters:

MAY JEHOVA RULE OVER THIS KINGDOM IN ALL HIS MIGHT.

This Synagogue was not the only one in Córdoba, although, together with the one in Toledo, it is the only one left standing after many vicissitudes.

After the expulsion of the Jews in 1492, the Synagogue was turned into a hospital for hydrophobics and in 1588 was given the name of St. Crispin, patron of the cobblers, because it was there that this trade brotherhood meetings were held.

THE RECONQUEST CHURCHES

Lambert, in his book «Gothic art in Spain» asserts that the existence of Gothic churches in Córdoba goes to prove that there was a true school of Gothic architecture in Andalucía.

When Fernando III, the Saint, reconquered Córdoba on 29th June 1236, he founded fourteen parish churches. The dates when they were built could be placed between the end of the XIII century and the beginning of the XIV century, and they all belong to the transition period from Romanic to Gothic together with some Arabic influence. Some authors have found Cistercian influence and others have found similarities with churches in Galicia. This is very possible given the influence of the Galician knights who came to conquer the city with the armies of Castilla and León. These churches were given a Baroque coating during the XVII and XVIII centuries.

All the Reconquest churches are of particular interest. As a rule, they were built with two aisles and a nave and a polygonal apse. Most outstanding of these churches are:

St. Nicholas de la Villa, which is an exception to the rule and has square apses. It has a beautiful octagonal tower decorated with a magnificent Arabic frieze and battlements adorned with the fleur-de-lys. It is the most representative and widely known of Córdoba's towers.

St. Peter's, which the Christian Arabs cathedral during the Mussulman rule. Here, the relics of the Holy Cordovan Martyrs are kept as well as valuable paintings.

Santiago's, which was built over an ancient mosque. It has a splayed portal and a gracious Gothic rose window in which are encrusted tiles.

St. Andrew's, which was built over the Christian Arabs' basilica which was dedicated to St. Zoilo in the time of the Mussulman rule and is in the silk embroiderers' quarter. Only the central apse, converted into Sacrarium, and its pure Gothic dome remain of the original building by St. Fernando.

The Magdalena, which, although possessing Gothic characteristics, appears more ancient. Its polygonal apses and specially its three splayed portals and pointed arches, are clearly seen from outside.

St. Laurence's, which has a splayed main entrance door, nearly covered by a XIV century portico above which is a marvellous rose window made up os six diminishing ribs which form the frame and a small central rose window, from which point small bows elegantly entwined and resting on slender little pillars.

St. Michael's. This church also possesses a magnificent rose window and beautiful side portal. The Baptistry chapel is of extremex interest.

St. Marina's, which has a splendid main façade with four buttresses lending it an appearance of a fortress. There are also three marvellous portals with slightly pointed arches, a central rose window and bulls eye between them.

The tower of San Nicolás de la Villa in the 19th century, according to an ▶ engraving by D. Roberts.

San Miguel Church. Side door of caliphal influence.

Santa Marina Church. North portal.

OTHER TEMPLES IN CORDOBA

As consequence of the reconquest of Córdoba in 1236, many convents were established, since then the Christian religion was at its strongest. Only the temples of some them (identical to the other churches built Fernando III) remain standing as with the present parish church of St. John's and Allsaints' (Trinidad) which was the convent of the Order of the Trinity and with St. Francis and St. Eulogio, which after having been uncloistered was turned into a parish church. This very interesting church belonged to the Franciscan convent of St. Peter, the Monarch, and was founded by Fernando III, the Saint, and is adorned with a multi-coloured, loud ornamentation. Paintings by Valdés Leal and Antonio del Castillo are held there. Next to it is the admirable mediaeval cloister of the convent, recently rescued for art reasons, and which is being restored as it should be.

St. Paul's. This is the most complete Reconquest church, according to Lampérez. He also affirms that it is the church with the strongest characteristics of Cordovan architecture in the XIII-XIV centuries. The original portal which gives on to alley leading to St. Paul's Street, is beautiful in the extreme and other which gives on to the Square of St. Salvador is also very interesting with its rather loud style and decorations. The Church has two aisles and one raised central nave with Arab style decorations on the panels and apses with ribbed domes reminiscent of Romanic adornments. Paintings by Antonio Palomino and figure sculptured by Duke Cornejo are kept there, also a gem of Spanish XVII century imagery: the Virgen of Sorrows by Juan de Mena.

There are other churches which hold great artistic interest: *St. Hipólito*, collegiate church founded in the XIV century, in commemoration of the Battle of the Salado. There lie Fernando IV and Alfonso XI in their sepulchres; *El Salvador and Santo Domingo de Silos*, built between 1564 and 1589 and is called of the «Company» because it belonged to the ancient Jesuit convent; *St. Victoria* with its pediment and neoclassic lines, was finished in 1788; *St. Raphael*, with a magnificent statue of he who gave his name to the church, Custodio of Córdoba by Gómez de Sandoval; *San Jacinto* with a marvellous Gothic portal with plateresque influence, statues in the typanum and side pilasters.

The Chapel of St. Bartholemew, the old and beautiful Gothic-Arabic building, merits a special visit. Before it is a horse-shoe arch resting on Roman shafts and Visigoth capitals. The portal is ogive, panel with Arabic adornments held up by Romanic capitals and a ribbed dome. It is adorned with Moorish plaster work which was carried out to perfection; the plinth is decorated with marvellous Dutch tiling and the floor is of XIV century tiles.

Arch of the ancient convent of San Francisco. ▶

Baroque portal of the church of San Pablo.

rior of San Hipólito Church.

Gothic portal of San Jacinto.

CONVENTS IN CORDOBA

There are many convents in Córdoba built at different points of the city after the Christian Reconquest. Over the centuries, until they were uncloistered in 1835, they were predominant and often used as a haven to kindle the artistic and cultural activities in the town.

Many of these places, where monks and nuns lived in communities fulfilling the doctrine of their Order, are still standing now. Here are a few which stand out for their historic and archeological value:

Convent of the Shod Carmelites with an excellent cloister and magnificent Arabic style church. Perhaps the high altar piece, painted by Valdés Leal in 1658, is the most outstanding work of art of this church and the best of this painter's works.

Convent of St. Agustín of the Dominican Order, which was built at the beginning of the XIV century. The apse, which belongs to this century, still remains with its delicate ribbing. A large reform was carried out in the XVI century giving the church plane the shape of a Latin cross and it was decorated in the plateresque style.

Convent of St. Isabel of the Franciscan nuns, was founded in 1491 and has a secluded entrance pation where tall cypruses give shade. There are held magnificent paintings and relics.

Convent of St. Cayetano of the Barefoot Carmelites, which was founded by San Juan de la Cruz in 1580. The whole of the church, which was built in Graeco-Roman style, is painted in oils representing scenes from the life of the holy founder and St. Teresa. These were painted by the Carmelite monk, Fray Juan del Santísimo Sacramento.

Monastery of St. Martha of the Hieronymite nuns which has a beautiful front patio. The church was built in 1471 and there is a delightful flowery Gothic portal.

Among other convents, the *Corpus Christi Convent* of the Dominican nuns should be visited if only to look at its enchanting cyprus shaded patio; the Convent of the *Padres de Gracia* of the Trinitarian monks, founded in 1607 and which holds some very interesting sculptures and holy relics; and the *Convent of Jesus Crucified* which was built in 1588. Its large patios with Visigoth and Arab capitals are extremely interesting and even more so the magnificent panelled ceilings. The ceiling over the nave of the church is quite exceptional and the one over the apse is beautifully decorated in a varation of colours.

98

Patio of Mercy, today the Palace of Provincial Deputation. ▶

Interior of the church of the convent of San Cayetano.

THE SQUARE OF SORROWS AND THE SQUARE OF THE FOAL

The Square of Sorrows, popularly known as the Square of the Capuchins, has two main characteristics: the seclusion and the silence. The definition given to Córdoba by Manuel Machado, is utterly valid here, «Roman and Moorish, silent Córdoba».

To the left one can see the eastern wall of the Convent of the Capuchins, built in the xvii century, and the long white wall of its outhouses. To the right, the Church of Sorrows and the Hospital of San Jacinto runs along the square. The figure of Our Lady of Sorrows, work of the sculptor from Granada, Juan Prieto (1719), is adored and constitutes one of the devotions which has found its way deep into the life of the Cordovans.

But it is the Crucifix, towering above the Square which gives it its exceptional air. The Crucifix is guarded by iron railings of medium height, put round in 1794. The plinth of the Crucifix is of stone from Cordoba's sierra and resting on this are two octagonal prisms, the higher one of which is adorned with the coat of arms of the Franciscan Order, the embrace between Christ and St. Francis and Our Lord's five wounds. The Cross rises above this and the figure of Christ of Revenge and Christ of Mercy. The people of the city call him Christ of Lanterns because of the eight lamps, like metal and glass flowers, which soften the morning calmness, the afternoon sun and the silence of the night with their oil lights.

The Square of the Foal is large and rectangular. Entering the Square from the old Calle de la Sillería, now called Romero Barros, the famous in which hold the name of the square is to the right in front of a «triunfo» to St. Raphael and to the left is the façade of what used to be the Hospital of Charity and the entrance to the Provincial Museums of Fine Arts and of Romero de Torres. In the centre, is an elegant stone fountain, built in 1577. Perfecting this beautiful combination is a rearing foal.

The name of the square is taken from the inn which already existed in the xv century and which still stands in its entirety. Vicente Espinel, refers to this inn in 1570 in his «Life of the page, Marcos de Obregón», as well as Miguel de Cervantes who also mentions the square in «Rinconete y Cortadillo» and in «El ingenioso hidalgo Don Quijote de la Mancha». Agujeros del Potro —needle manufacturers— were three of those who tossed Sancho Panza in the blanket at the Inn and even the innkeeper of this famous book had learnt his mischief here in this square according to Cervantes.

During the xvi and xvii centuries, the Square of the Foal, was a stopping for the nomads, place of commerce, gamblers' den, travellers' resting place, traders meeting place and centre of information from all those travelling round Spain in search of glory or fortune. Now, it is still almost intact and it seems that time has stopped still there.

A view of the Colt Inn. ▶

Archeological Museum. Roman mosaic.

Façade of San Lorenzo Church. ▶

Portal of the San Bartolomé chapel. ◄

La Merced Church. Baroque faÍade (18th C.).

Cordova to die.

Patio of the Colt Inn.

MUSEUMS IN CORDOBA

In the Square of Jerónimo Páez is the Archeological Museum, which is considered to be one of the best in Spain and exceptional centre of culture. The beautiful and fitting arrangement of its extraordinary collections make the visitor gape and fills him spiritually and makes him nostalgic. The archeological relics could not be more attractively presented and better placed than among its enchanting patios, gardens, halls and galleries.

This museum has in its possession articles of great value, among which, merits special reference the stone lion found in New Carthage; several Roman statues, like a head of Germanic and a bust of the Emperor Commodo; Visigoth archivolts and adornments; painted brick and capital of the Evangelists from the same age; Visigoth crosses from the treasury of Torredonjimeno; decorative reliefs, capitals and buttress in the style of the Caliph age; bronze deer found in the ruins of Madinat al-Zahra; curb of an Arab well; golden shaded tile from the chapel of St. Bartholomew; figures of an Annunciation from the xv century; Roman mosaics, amphora, capitals, coins which are unequalled.

The Provincial Museum of Fine Arts is in the Square of the Foal, on the site of the old Hospital of Charity. It has been described as a poetical garden filled with statues. In this museum are some excellent paintings of which should be mentioned «San Nicolás de Bari», by Pedro de Córdoba; «Virgen con el niño», by Pedro Romana; «Flagelación» and «Cristo a la columna», by Alejo Fernández; «David victorioso», by Zambrano; «La Trinidad», by Agustín del Castillo; «St. Paul», «Imposición de la casulla a San Ildefonso» and «Crucifix», by fray Juan del Santísimo Sacramento; «Birth of San Pedro Nolasco», by Cobo-Guzmán; «Virgen de los plateros», by Juan Valdés Leal; «San Jerónimo», by Zurbarán; «Santa Inés», by Bernabé de Ayala; «Adoration of the shepherds», by José Sarabia; «The Holy Family», by Andrés Pérez; «Crucifix with the Virgen and St. John», «Christ after death adored by angels», «St. Peter and St. Paul» and others by Antonio del Castillo who is considered as the best of Cordovan painters in the xvii century; «Charles IV» and «María Luisa», by Goya; and paintings, by Eugenio Lucas, Rosales, Mengs, Romero Barros and others. Lastly let us mention a large hall dedicated to the unrivalled Cordovan sculptor, Mateo Inurria.

In the same building is the Museum of Julio Romero de Torres where many of his canvasses can be seen: «Chiquita buena», «Oranges and lemons», «La chiquita piconera», «Angeles y Fuensanta», «El poema de Córdoba», «La Virgen de los Faroles», «El martirio de Santa Inés», «Viva el pelo», «La magdalena», «El pecado», «La nieta de la Trini», «Ofrenda al arte del toreo», «Cante jondo», «Samaritana», etc.

The City Historical Museum, in the Calahorra and the Mosque Museum in the street «Comedias» are also of great interest.

In the Square of the Bulas is the Municipal Taurine Museum and Typical Arts Museum which hold souvenirs of Cordovan bull-fighters and the art of the Cordovans, leather embossers and silversmiths.

113

Patio of the Provincial Archeological Museum.

Archeological Museum. Iberian lion of New Carteya.

Museum of Fine Arts. Retable of the Flagelation, by Alfonso de Aguilar (16th C.).

Museum of Fine Arts. *Rest in the Flight to Egypt*, by José Ribera.

Museum of
Fine Arts.
San Pablo,
canvas by
A n t o n i o
del Castillo.

THE SQUARE OF THE CORREDERA

The Square of the Corredera is an enormous rectangle with a lower porticoed gallery which runs right round the square except on the south side where there is only a very short span. The arcade, and rounded arches over pillars support three storeys os rectangular and symmetrical gaps and prolonged iron balconies where multicoloured flowers grow and creepers which almost hide the old balcony railings. The combination of stone, lime and brick here is strikingly harmonised.

The present organisation of the Square dates back to the last third of the XVII century, when it was transformed by the mayor, don Francisco Ronquillo Briceño. The popularly called Houses of Dona María Jacinta in the south-west corner and the old prison, built in 1583 and next to the above mentioned Houses contrasting with the rest of the Square, are still conserved from olden times. It is in this square that bull fights are held and other shows and spectacles. This is how the square got its name.

Recent archeological finds discovered under the floor of the square —valuable Roman mosaics on show in the Fortress of the Catholic Kings— together with other finds, prove that this was the main grand entrance to Cordoba's amphitheatre.

THE ALLEY OF FLOWERS

The Alley of Flowers is in the laberinthic old part of Córdoba around the Mosque. The Street Comedias has to be crossed to reach the alley. The city's theatre was in Comedias during the XVI century. The old capital and pillar set in the white corner seems to indicate the entrance to the alley. Without the visitor realising it, the Alley of Flowers appears before him and like those hidden mill on the rivers in the Sierra, have an irrestible attraction which draws him into its beautiful and dream-like precinct.

Carnations, roses, jasmins, geraniums, stocks, nightshade, all Andalusian flowers rivalling to be admired by the visitor. These flowers shoot forth, grow and die in the most unlikely pots, from earthenware to glass, passing through aluminium and tin. Nobody touches or even dares to cut these flowers, which embellish the material of their pots with their noble beauty.

The roofs, wrought iron over the windows and the front door gratings all take us back to the time of the House Austria in Spain, for it is to this age that this street belongs. If the visitor were to look back towards the entrance of the street from the wider part, he would see the Mosque tower rising from between the walls and arches to be outlined against the blue sky. From time to time the sound, the solemn ringing of its bronze bells, put the finishing touch to an almost perfect dream.

Corredera Square.
Aerial view of

CORDOVAN PATIOS

The Cordovan patios originated during the period of the Romans. They lead directly on the rooms and galleries of the lower and higher floors of the buildings by arches or windows and balconies or by railing with porches and small roofs where jasmins, bellwort and orange and lemon treas climb. The Cordovan habit of planting the two latter against the walls so that their leaves spread across the whiteness of the walls is extremely enchanting. The purple and gold of the oranges and lemons contrast beautifully with the whiteness and the intoxicating perfume of orange blossom perfects the whole breathtaking sight.

The Arab taste for the seclusion of the family gave rise to privacy in the Cordovan patios which lasted even when Renaissance influence for more open type building was introduced. It was during the Arab epoch when the grating over the front doors were introduced through which one could look at the street. But this did make the patios lose their simplicity and privacy although these gratings were not totally fitting for the entrance to the patios. The Mussulman influence still lasts especially with the more popular patios, and the houses have their small doors with a narrow entrance to amazing brightness inside. These are enjoyed and looked after by the inhabitants of the house.

The patios in Córdoba are so numerous and so varied that a superficial description cannot be made, although all those belonging to the old palaces, mansions and museums can be pointed out as interesting and mention those belonging to private houses because they are more difficult to find but merit a special visit.

Among many others the following are well worth seeing: Calle «Badanas», 15: of several bodies with three stories in the background which end in small arches. This one is considered to be the most beautiful; «Albucasis», 6: with an octagonal shaped bowl around its central fountain; «San Basilio» 27: small with wood balconies; «San Basilio» 50: with a tremendous variety of plants and flowers displayed on trellises and in almost a thousand pots; «Duartas» 4: with a well to the left, lower and higher galleries and long balcony; «Enmedio» 25: with brick arches which are whitewashed, well and country style cooker; «Enmedio» 29: with a portal of three whitewashed arches, pillars and capitals; «Parras» 4: in a house built in 1589; «Montero» 12: a combination of communicating patios with brick arches; «Cristo» 14: with two precincts joined by a passage covered with plant pots; «Velasco» 3: with plinths, pillars and Roman, Visigoth and Arabic capitals; «San Juan de Palomares» 11: long and stone floored, where there is an arch where the smallest plants of all the patios drape; «Aguas» 2: enchantingly irregular; «Aguas» 3: with arches, railing and lamps; and «Siete Revueltas» 3: with trellises in front of white walls and an abundance of geraniums. Finally, the patios in «Plaza de las Tazas» 11 should be mentioned with its intricate entrances, well, large earthen jar set in the wall and a palm tree which softly fans the wavy and oblique line of the roofs.

◀ The enchanting Little Square of the Flowers.

A typical patio in Cordova.

Main patio of the Palace of the Marquis of Viana.

PALACES AND MANOR HOUSES

Magnificent palaces and ancestral manor houses standing in the Squares and hidden streets are an example of the successive artistic and architectural styles over the centuries in Córdoba.

The *Palace of the Provincial Council* should be particularly referred to. It is in Columbus Square and was built over what was originally the Convent of the Mercedarians. This building has several patios among which the Renaissance one and the one at the entrance with white marble, central fountain, large arcades and excellent balconies which with the stairs, make up a beautiful combination. The best of all is the Baroque church with the arms of the transept covered with half oranges. The stautes at the high altar are of great importance and are the work of Gómez de Sandoval. The paintings are by Cobo de Guzmán and the Crucifix from the XIV century is doubtlessly the oldest in Córdoba. The façade is extremely interesting. It is large and painted and adorned profusely and brightly in Baroque style. The portal of the church is loud and dates back to 1745.

The building of the *Music Conservatory and School of Dramatic Art*, educational centre in the old rebuilt palace of Marqués de la Fuensanta del Valle, has a beautiful patio and a magnificent theatre. The portal is still in perfect condition. It was built in 1551 and is a living sample of the plateresque style although slightly reminiscent of the Gothic style. The *School of Applied Arts and Artistic Trades* established in the palace of the Dukes of Hornachuelos, has a magnificent XVII century staircase, artistic show cases and enchanting galleries and gardens. The *Casa de los Páez*, where the Archeological Museum is established, is fascinatingly beautiful with its combination of patios, gardens, galleires, fountains and mosaics. The façade of this building, built by Hernán Ruiz and Sebastian de Peñarredonda in 1540, gives an inkling of what can be expected inside. The portal of this palace is richly decorated with reliefs, doric pillars and figures of warriors. A wide cornice completes the building at the top. This is adorned with fine lattice work.

Then there is the *Palace of the Marqués de Viana*, the ancestral home of the Villaseca. One enters through a XVII century patio where there is rich and multi-coloured panelling over the staircase, then there are halls, and a very replete library with select venatic subjects.. This palace has a very valuable collection of embossed leather and tiles, some rare examples from the XIII century, and Cordovan silver work with some very important filigree jewels. This building has a total of fourteen patios, all of which are extraordinarily beautiful with box-trees, cipruses, garden orange trees, trained and shoots.

The following houses are worthy of a visit: *de las Campanas*, *Indiano*, *Marqueses de El Carpio*, *Villalones*, *Hernán Pérez de Oliva* and *Duque de Medina Sidonia*.

Portal of the house of the Ceas or of the Indiano (15th C.).

The harmonious façade of the house of the Villalones (1560).

Archeological Museum. Head of the young Druso, from Puente Genil. ▶

Archeological Museum. Bronze deer, from Madinat al-Zahra.

Colt Square, with the façade of the Fine Arts Museum.

Romero de Torres Museum. *The little charcoal maker,* canvas by Julio Romero de Torres.

Fine Arts Museum. *Christ on the column*, by Alejo Fernández.

Fine Arts Museum. *Calvary*, by Antonio del Castillo (1645).

◀Patio of the Municipal Taurine and Typical Arts Museum.

A beautiful Cordovan patio, on Badanas Street.

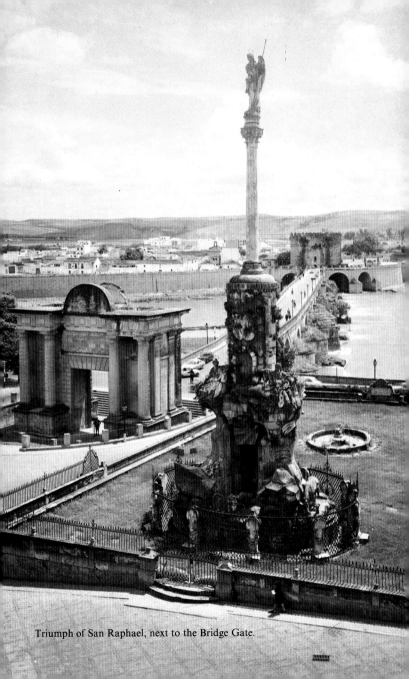

Triumph of San Raphael, next to the Bridge Gate.

◀ Monument to Manolete in Santa Marina Square.

The tranquil street of the Judíos.

Motif of the Cordovan Holy Week.

Girls from Cordova at the Fair grounds.

José Antonio Square, present day urban center.

THE TRIUMPHAL STATUES OF ST. RAPHAEL

The popular devotion to the Archangel St. Raphael, goes back over many centuries. He is the guardiam angel of Córdoba and in the XVII century statues were built like those that can still be seen on the Roman bridge by Bernabé Gómez del Río in 1651 and the one at the top of the cathedral tower by Pedro de Paz in 1664.

This already special devotion was accentuated in the XVIII century during which century most of the monuments involving in one way or another, the archangel, were called by the people «Triumphal Statues of St. Raphael».

The «Triumphal Statue» by antonomasia is the one whose graceful silhouette rises above the esplanade between the Bridge Gate, the Seminary and the Mosque. It was built between 1765 and 1781 by MiguelVerdiguier at the order of the cathedral chapter. The plinth is made of an anormous mass of stone and in the hollows can be seen represented fauna and floraand Cordovan products. Above this stone rest statues of St. Bárbara, St. Acisclo and St. Victoria. There are also some relics of saints, the sepulchre of the bishop, Don Pascual and a delicate pillar on which rests the figure of St. Raphael.

All the Triumphal statues have a modillion on which reads the oathmade, according to tradition, by the archangel when he appeared to Father Roelas: I SWEAR ON OATH AND CHRIST CRUCIFIED THAT I AM RAPHAEL? THE ANGEL WHOM GOD CHARGED WITH GUARDING THIS CITY.

MONUMENTS TO ILLUSTRIOUS CORDOVANS

Just a short commentary of famous names given to the world of letters and art by Córdoba would need more space than can be dedicated to this subject here. An enumeration of those main ones to whom the city has dedicated a commerative monument is all that can be written.

In the poetical Street of the Ramparts there are monuments dedicated to the great philosopher of the classic world, Lucio Anneo Séneca by the sculptor Ruiz Olmos and to Averroes, one of greatest of Moslem philosophers by Pablo Tusti. Nearby, in front of the arches in the Puerta de Sevilla there is another magnificent statue by Ruiz Olmos of the polygraph, Aben Házam who was a prodigious Nispano-Moslem writer.

A statue, also by Ruiz Olmos, of the great poet, don Luis de Góngora y Argote, stands in the Square of the Trinity, and in the gardens of the Victory, can be seen the monument to the Duke of Rivas by Mariano Benlliure.

Osio who was the key figure during the first centuries of Christianism; Maimónides, the greatest figure among the Jews in Spain; don Gonzalo Fernández de Córdoba, the Great Captain; Julio Romero de Torres, painter of the Cordovan lady; the great bull fighter, Manuel Rodríguez «Manolete»; and many other universal Cordovans who have been given a monument and gala by their place of birth.

Triumph of San Raphael in Company Square, by Alonso Pérez and Juan Jiménez (1736).

Aguayos Square. Triumph of San Raphael (1763).

Monument to Maimonedes.

TYPICAL SPOTS

Córdoba lends itself for walking and looking at the typical corners which are unending. Besides the grandiose and beautiful historical and archeological examples in the city, these corners provide the perfecting touch to the enchanting old capital of the Caliphs.

It is even more enchanting the feel of mystery and evocation during a walk at night. The following places would be suggested:

«Calle de la Luna» which leads one from the Ramparts through a maze of little narrow streets right into the Jewish quarter. «Callejas de la Hoguera» recently recovered when an old house in the middle of it was demolished. The old house prevented access to the Callejas. «Calleja de Pedro Jiménez» or the «Rincones del Oro», which ends in a small XVII century square where only few people can barely fit. This place is so extraordinarily small that the visitor can prove it for himself by folding a handkerchief diagonally and then touching the walls on either side with the corners of the handkerchief. «Plaza de Séneca» and «Calleja de Junio Gallon», are also interesting places. «Cuesta de Peramato» with its evocative steps and long trained cypresses

The «Calle de la Feria» and «San Fernando» the main street where rows of orange trees all along it contrast with the whiteness of its pavements. In the highest part is a magnificent fountain built in 1796 with two spouts from which is a constant flow of water. Towards the middle of this street is the famous arch of the «wicket gate» opening in a horseshoe in the XIV century in order to make transit easier between the «Almedina» and the «Axerquía».

Going through the arch of the «wicket gate» and along the «Calle Cabezas» an extremely narrow street can be found, with its entrance guarded by grating and seven arches of stone work running from wall to wall. According to an inscription written under the auspices of the great investigator, don Ramón Menéndez Pidal, the literary and popular traditions affirm that in the centre of those arches hung the heads of the seven infant princes of Lara.

The «Cuestas del Bailío», «Plaza de la Fuenseca», «La Lagunilla», «Compás de San Francisco», «Arco de Caballerizas Reales» and the quarter of the «Old Fortress» are also most evocative.

Pedro Jiménez Street. ▶

The popular small street of Hoguera.

CORDOBA TODAY

Very aware of its historical destiny and responsibility, Córdoba advances calmly and unhesitatingly through Time, with is old wisdom in perfect harmony with the liveliest and modern tendencies.

In the centre of the city, which is now the Square of José Antonio, formerly «de las Tendillas» some very modern buildings have been erected mingling with the old which the city has contributed over the centuries. The use of old Cordovan resources contribute to the harmony. These resources never fail when it is a matter of keeping the architecture uniform. Because of this, the rows of acacias and orange trees in the square and street of «Claudio Marcelo» are decisive; the awnings which provide shade and coll the street of «Gondomar» in summer and the typical clock which delights visitors from the top of a building in «Tendillas», because instead of chiming at the hour it plays parts of a «solear» on the guitar.

Córdoba is being given a face lift with new and confortable buildings with all the latest technical demands although in the wide artistic area no transformation has been allowed in order not to spoil or lose its authentic breath of olden days. Daring buildings have built, where together with the hard cement work, iron, steel and aluminium grow colourful geraniums and roses which soften and beautify these modern materials making them blend into the typical look of the region with their simple green stalks and covering them with their leaves.

Houses, trees, flowers and sky all beldn together in the wide avenues of the «Conde de Vallellano» and the «República Argentina»; in the square of «Colón» and in the avenue of «América», in the avenues of the «Alcázar», of «Medina Azahara», «Generalísimo», «Cervantes», «Gran Capitán», del «Corregidor», of «Granada» and of «Cádiz».

Its «Gran Vía Parque» must be mentioned. This is crossed by the avenue to the «airport», the first fruit of a grandiose urban road network, the main building of which is the very modern «Plaza de Toros» and the «Parque José Cruz Conde» where stands the new and elegant Provincial Hospital considered to be one of the best in Europe.

Another excellent of modern buildings in Córdoba is the «Working University» of Onésimo Redondo, with its grandiose style. The main pavillion, now the church, with its beautiful mosaics and stained glass windows is admirable.

Partial view of the Conde de Vallelano Avenue.

Partial view of the Labor University.

The National Parador of Tourism, «La Arruzafa».

THE OUTSKIERTS OF CORDOBA

At the foot of the Sierra, where the city of Córdoba lies, are beautiful buildings dotted around and completely isolated. They contrast with the green of the gardens and orchards. The Sierra forms part and parcel of the life in Córdoba and this has been understood by its people over the years, people usually given to seclusion and devotion. It has some very interesting places.

The Hermitages. The hermitages were established in the Sierra right from the very beginning of Christianism. The Moslems religious tolerance over the years of their reign, let these Christian places stand and even allowed to become churches and convents. These original hermitages are worthy of visiting because of, among other reasons, the contrast clearly seen between the hard and isolated life of the hermits in their individual houses and the beautiful view of the far off city. The church which crowns and seems to guard over these buildings, was built in the XVIII century. In 1929, an outstanding monument was erected there to the Sacred Heart of Jesús by Coullant Valera, and which can be seen from far away.

Monastery of San Jerónimo. It lies very near to the ruins of Madinat al-Zahra and was founded in 1408 in the orchard called «Valparaíso» donated by doña Inés de Pontevedra, mother of the Wader of the Pages. It was founded by a Portuguese monk, fray Vasco de Sousa. The most important work of this monastery corresponds to the time of its foundation when it was built in the Gothic style with an strikingly beautiful Gothic cloister which is, without a doubt, the best in Córdoba. Since its foundation in 1835, the monastery has belonged to the Order of the Jerónimos. It is now the property of the Marqueses of Merit, who have embellished and furnished it, thus increasing its value with precious paintings and jewels.

Santo Domingo de Escala Coeli. A Dominican convent at 7 kilometres from Córdoba right in the sierra. It was founded by San Alvaro de Córdoba, whose relics are still preserved together with souvenirs and religious articles. The convent was enlarged by fray Luis de Granada, who wrote many of his works here, mainly «Book of Prayer and Meditation». The church was restored in XVIII century and is painted and adorned with scenes from the life of San Alvaro and scenes of the history of the Dominican Order. On the first Sundays of spring a popular pilgrimage is held to the sanctuary.

Our Lady of Linares. Built 7 kilometres from Córdoba in the place where, according to tradition, St. Fernando camped when he was preparing to conquer the city and it is said the figure of the Holy Virgen standing there and revered, was brought by the Holy King on the back of his saddle. The small chapel dates beck to the XIV century. Here also a pilgrimage is held during the first days of May.

Principal façade and cloister of the San Jerónimo Monastery, in the Sierra of Cordova (15th C.).

MADINAT AL-ZAHRA AND MADINAT AL-ZAHIRA

Madinat al-Zahra, the popular Medina Azahara, was built by the caliph Abd al-Rahman III at 5 kilometres from Córdoba. The building was carried out with the money bequeathed by the favourite al-Zahra. Building was started in 352 of the hegira (936 a.d.) and took 25 years to finish. Abd al-Rahman III's successors enlarged and embellished its ornamentation and its gardens. In spite of this, the beautiful town suffered more than any other, the political changes and in 1010, after only 74 years, it was destroyed and plundered by the Berbers. In 1236, when Córdoba was conquered by Fernando III, the Saint, only a reminiscence of Madinat al-Zahra remained and the material of its ruins were used to build palaces, churches and convents. In 1853, Pedro de Madrazo identified the remains and in 1923 the whole place was declared as a National Monument.

The site of the city is almost rectangular and is terraced in order to cope with the mountain slope and each terrace is seaparated by long walls. The highest part was where the palaces were built, in the middle part were the orchards and gardens and in the lower part was the main mosque, houses, workshops and other buildings. There is still a wide area where the mounds formed by the old rubbish heaps and earth which time has accumulated and which indicate clearly were many of the buildings stood and where excavation has not yet been carried out.

The visitor is given an idea of the magnificence of the city just walking round its halls and patios since paintings, plinths and tiles as well as fragments of pillars, shafts, pedestals and white marble capitals beautifully carved and corresponding to the Corinthian and composite orders, still remain.

Where there is true example of Madinat al-Zahra's beauty and harmonious proportions is in the building discovered in 1944 where so much material was found so as to make it possible to make a faithful restoration. It is a magnificent hall which was used for audiences and receptions of the Caliph Abd al-Rahman III and his successors and from the inscriptions which not only refer to dates but also to the names of the artists who built, it, it can be realised that the building was finished in 156 to 957. The profusion of pillars, capitals, arcades, plinths, wall facings show us the Syrian and Bizantine influence in all its splendour on the Cordovan architects which is the most beautiful of all Spanish caliph art.

This cannot be ended without dedicating something to Madinat al-Zahra, the courtly town founded by Almanzor. It is difficult to fix its exact position although it is known that it was built on the right bank of the Guadalquivir and that as the town grew its streets and houses reached the outskirts of Córdoba. It was destroyed and plundered in 1009 and with its destruction ended the dynasty of the amirs.

Entrance arch of the Royal Salón of Madinat al-Zahra. ▶

An ornamental motif at Madinat al-Zahra.

INFORMACION PRACTICA DE CORDOBA

La mayor parte de estos datos han sido facilitados por la Delegación Provincial de Información y Turismo de Córdoba. Información puesta al día el 30-1-71.

INFORMATION PRATIQUE SUR CORDOUE

La plupart de ces données ont été fournies par la Délégation Provinciale d'Information et de Tourisme de Cordoue. Information mise à jour le 30-1-71.

PRACTICAL INFORMATION OF CORDOBA

Most of this information has been facilitated by the Córdoba Provincial Delegation of Information and Tourism. Information written up on 30th January, 1971.

PRAKTISCHE HINWELSE VON CORDOBA

Die meisten der hier gemachten Angaben sind freundlicherweise von der Delegación Provincial de Información y Turismo von Córdoba zur Verfügung gestellt worden.

A CÓRDOBA

¡OH EXCELSO MVRO, OH TORRES CORONADAS
DE HONOR, DE MAJESTAD, DE GALLARDIA!
¡OH GRAN RIO, GRAN REY DE ANDALVCIA,
DE ARENAS NOBLES, YA QVE NO DORADAS!

¡OH FERTIL LLANO, OH SIERRAS LEVANTADAS,
QVE PRIVILEGIA EL CIELO Y DORA EL DIA!
¡OH SIEMPRE GLORÏOSA PATRIA MIA,
TANTO POR PLVMAS CVANTO POR ESPADAS!

¡SI ENTRE AQVELLAS RVINAS Y DESPOJOS
QVE ENRIQVECE GENIL Y DAVRO BAÑA
TV MEMORIA NO FVÉ ALIMENTO MIO,

NVNCA MEREZCAN MIS AVSENTES OJOS
VER TV MVRO, TVS TORRES Y TV RIO,
TV LLANO Y SIERRA, OH PATRIA, OH FLOR DE ESPAÑA!

Don Luis de Góngora y Argote

Córdoba, centro de Andalucía y regada por el Guadalquivir, tiene una extensión de 13.716,60 Km² y una población de 800.000 habitantes. El trigo, la viña y sobre todo el olivo caracterizan su panorama agrícola. Las minas de hulla de Belmez y de Peñarroya-Pueblo Nuevo y las de potasio y bismuto, en Pozoblanco, tienen gran importancia. Destacan como centros industriales: Córdoba, Palma del Río, Priego y Puente Genil. Su clima es continental y seco, alcanzando elevadas temperaturas durante el verano. Baena, Luque, Cabra, Lucena, Aguilar, Priego, Bujalance, Montoro y Fuente Obejuna son poblaciones de gran historia. El cante y el baile flamenco tienen en Córdoba uno de sus centros de origen y de difusión más importantes.
La capital es una de las más bellas ciudades andaluzas. Cuenta con monumentos de renombre universal, entre los que destaca sobre todos la Mezquita, joya máxima de arte árabe. En el ámbito artístico son famosos los Museos de Julio Romero de Torres, Bellas Artes y Arqueológico.
Su mesa es de recio sabor, como lo atestigua la olla cordobesa.
Sus vinos de Montilla y Moriles son famosos en el mundo.

La province de Cordoue, au centre de l'Andalousie et arrosée par le Guadalquivir, a une superficie de 13.716,60 km², et une population de 800.000 habitants. Le blé, la vigne, et surtout l'olivier, caractérisent son paysage agricole. Les mines de houille de Belmez et de Peñarroya-Pueblo Nuevo et celles de potassium et de bismuth, à Pozoblanco, ont une grande importance. Les principaux centres industriels sont: Cordoue, Palma del Río, Priego et Puente Genil. Le climat y est continental et sec, il atteint en été des températures élevées. Baena, Luque, Cabra, Lucena, Aguilar, Priego, Bujalance, Montoro, et Fuente Obejuna sont des villes hautement historiques. En ce qui concerne le chant et la danse «flamenco», Cordoue est un de leurs centres d'origine et de difusion les plus importants.

La capitale est l'une des plus belles villes andalouses. Elle a des monuments d'une célébrité universelle, parmi lesquels se distingue par-dessus tout la Mosquée, le plus beau joyau de l'art arabe. Dans le domaine artistique, le musée de Julio Romero de Torres, Beaux-Arts et Archéologique un grand renom.
La cuisine est très épicée, ainsi qu'en témoigne le pot-au-feu cordouan.
Les vins de Montilla et de Moriles sont célèbres dans le monde entier.

Córdoba is the centre of Andalucía and is irrigated by the Guadalquivir River. Its area is 13.716,60 km² and it has 800,000 inhabitants. Wheat, grapes and especially olives form the main part of its agriculture. The coal mines in Belmez and Peñarroya-Pueblo Nuevo and the potassium and bismuth mines are of great importance. The principal industrial zones are: Córdoba, Palma del Río, Priego and Puente Genil. The climate is continental and dry; temperatures are extremely high in summer. Baena, Luque, Cabra, Lucena, Aguilar, Priego, Bujalance, Montoro and Fuente Obejuna are all towns of great historical background. Córdoba is one of the places where the Flamenco singing and dancing originated and where it is most widely diffused.
The capital is one of the most beautiful Andalucian cities. The monuments there, are worls famous and among the most outstanding is the Mosque, a gem of Arabic art. The Julio Romero de Torres, Fine Arts and Archeological Museum are famous in artistic circles.
The typical food is very strong in flavour as is proved by the Cordoban «olla».
The wine from Montilla and Moriles is world famous.

Córdoba, das Zentrum Andalusiens, hat eine Ausdehnung von 13.716,60 km² und 800.000 Einwohner. Es wird von dem Guadalquivir bewässert. Weizen, Wein und vor allem Oliven bestimmen die Landwirtschaft. Sehr Wichtig sind die Steinkohlen-

minen von Belmez und Peñarroya-Pueblo Nuevo ebenso wie die Kali— und Bismut-Minen ib Pozoblanco. Hervorstechende Industriezentren sind Córdoba, Palma del Rio, Priego und Puente Genil. Córdoba hat trockenes Kontinentalklima mit hohen Temperaturen im Sommer. Baena, Luque, Cabra, Lucena, Aguilar, Priego, Bujalance, Montoro und Fuente Obejuna sind Orte mit großer Geschichte. Córdoba ist einer der wixhtigsten Augangspunkte und Zentren der Verbreitung des Cante jondo und des Flamenco-Tanzes.

Die Hauptstadt ist eine der schönsten Städte Andalusiens. Sie besitzt Bauwerke von weltweitem Ruf, unter welchen vor allem die Mezquita hervorsticht, die höchste Vollendung arabischer Kunst. Auf künstlerischem Gebiet sind vor allem berühmt das Museum Julio Romero de Torres, das der Schönen Künste und das Archäologische Museum.

Die Küche Córdobas ist einfach und kräftig, was der kordobesische Eintopf beweist. Die Weine von Montilla und Moriles sind weltbekannt.

CONJUNTO MONUMENTAL

MEZQUITA-CATEDRAL. *Horas de visita:* Mañana (todo el año): de 10'30 a 13'30. Tarde: enero, febrero, noviembre y diciembre, de 15'30 a 17'30; marzo y octubre, de 15'30 a 18'00; abril, de 15'30 a 19; mayo y agosto, de 16'00 a 19'30; septiembre, de 16'00 a 19'00; junio y julio, de 16'00 a 20'00. Las horas de culto quedan excluidas de visitas turísticas.

Precio de entrada: 20 pesetas; niños, 10 pesetas; máquinas fotográficas, 10 pesetas.

MUSEO PROVINCIAL DE BELLAS ARTES. *Horas de visita:* Mañana: enero a junio y ¢eptiembre a diciembre, de 10'00 a 13'30; julio y agosto, y todos los domingos y festivos del año, de 10'00 a 14'00. Tarde: enero, noviembre y diciembre, de 15'30 a 17'00; febrero, de 15'30 a 17'30; marzo y octubre, de 15'30 a 18'00; abril, mayo, junio y septiembre, de 16'00 a 19'00. Permanece cerrado durante las tardes de los meses de julio y agosto, y durante todo el día en las siguientes fechas: 1 de enero, 24 de octubre, 25 de diciembre y el Viernes Santo.

Precio de entrada: 5 pesetas; domingos, gratis.

MUSEO DE JULIO ROMERO DE TORRES. Instalado en el mismo edificio que el anterior. Plaza del Potro.

Horas de visita: Las mismas que para el Museo Provincial de Bellas Artes.

Entrada gratuita.

MUSEO ARQUEOLOGICO PROVINCIAL. *Horas de visita:* Mañana (todo el año): de 10'00 a 13'30. Tarde (cerrado los meses de julio y agosto y todos los domingos y festivos del año): enero a abril y septiembre a diciembre, de 16'00 a 18'00; mayo y junio, de 17'00 a 19'00.

Precio entrada: 20 pesetas.

MUSEO MUNICIPAL TAURINO Y DE ARTES TIPICAS. *Horas de visita:* Mañana (todo el año): de 9'30 a 13'30. Tarde: de 1 de mayo al 30 de septiembre, de 17'00 a 20'00; de 1 de octubre al 30 de abril, de 16'00 a 19'00.

Precio de entrada: 5 pesetas.

PUENTE ROMANO

MURALLAS

TORRE DE LA CALAHORRA. Construcción árabe, situada junto al Puente Romano, en la margen izquierda del Guadalquivir.

Horas de visita: Mañana (todo el año): de 9'30 a 13'30. Tarde: de 1 de mayo a 30 de septiembre, de 17'00 a 20'00; de 1 de octubre a 30 de abril, de 16'00 a 19'00.

Precio de entrada: 5 pesetas.

TORRE DE LA MALMUERTA.

PUERTA DEL PUENTE.

ALCAZAR DE LOS REYES CRISTIANOS. *Horas de visita:* Mañana (todo el año): de 9'30 a 13'30. Tarde: de 1 de mayo a 30 de septiembre, de 17'00 a 20'00; de 1 de octubre a 30 de abril, de 16'00 a 19'00; jardines iluminados, de 1 de mayo a 30 de septiembre, de 22'00 a 1'00.

Precio de entrada: 10 pesetas; uso de máquinas fotográficas, 10 pesetas; visita a los jardines iluminados, 5 pesetas.

SINAGOGA.

CAPILLA DE SAN BARTOLOME.

IGLESIA DE SANTA MARINA DE AGUAS SANTAS.

IGLESIA DE SAN MIGUEL.

IGLESIA CONVENTUAL DE SAN PABLO.

IGLESIA DE SAN NICOLAS.

IGLESIA DE SAN LORENZO.

IGLESIA DE LA MAGDALENA.

COLEGIO DE LA COMPAÑIA.

PALACIO DE LA DIPUTACION.

CASA DEL INDIANO.

PALACIO DE LOS MARQUESES DE VIANA.

PALACIO DE LOS MARQUESES DEL CARPIO.

CASA DE LOS VILLALONES.

CALLEJA DE LAS FLORES.

PLAZA DE LOS DOLORES.

MONUMENTO A MANOLETE.

ZOCO. En la casa llamada antiguamente de «Las Bulas», edificio del siglo XVI. Mercado de artesanía. Tiene entrada por las calles de Judíos y Averroes.

POSADA DEL POTRO.

PLAZA DE LA CORREDERA.

PATIOS. Uno de los atractivos de mayor interés que conserva Córdoba son los patios de sus viejas casas. Compiten en sabor y belleza los de las casas señoriales y los más humildes y populares.

MOLINOS ARABES. Aguas abajo del Puente Romano se conservan diversos molinos, entre los que destacan los llamados de la Albolafia, de Enmedio y el Molino de Papel.

LAS ERMITAS. A 10 kilómetros de la capital.
MONASTERIO DE SAN JERONIMO DE
VALPARAISO. En las afueras de la capital
y cerca de Medina Azahara.
RUINAS DE MEDINA AZAHARA. Situadas a
pocos kilómetros de la capital.
Horas de visita: Mañana (todo el año): de
9'30 a 13'30. Tardes: de 16 de marzo a 15 de
septiembre, de 16 a 19'30; de 16 de septiembre a 15 de marzo, de 15 a 17'30.
Precio de entrada: 15 pesetas.

ENSEMBLE MONUMENTAL

MOSQUEE-CATHEDRALE. Heures de visite:
*Matin (toute l'année): de 10h 30 à 13h 30.
Après-midi: janvier, février, novembre et décembre, de 15h 30 à 17h 30; mars et octobre,
de 15h 30 à 18h; avril, de 15h 30 à 19h; mai
et août, de 16h à 19h 30; septembre, de
16h à 19h; juin et juillet, de 16h à 20h. Les
heures de culte sont exclues des visites
touristiques. Prix de l'entrée: 20 pesetas;
enfants: 10 pesetas; appareils photographiques: 10 pesetas.*
MUSEE PROVINCIAL DES BEAUX-ARTS.
Heures de visite: *Matin: de janvier à juin
et de septembre à décembre, de 10h à 13h 30;
juillet et août, et toute l'année dimanches et
jours fériés, de 10h à 14h. Après-midi:
janvier, novembre et décembre, de 15h 30 à
17h; février, de 15h 30 à 17h 30; mars et
octobre, de 15h 30 à 18h; avril, mai, juin et
septembre, de 16h à 19h. Reste fermé
l'après-midi pendant les mois de juillet et
août, et toute la journée les jours suivants:
1er janvier, 24 octobre, 25 décembre, Ven-
dredi Saint. Prix de l'entrée: 5 pesetas;
dimanches: gratuit.*
MUSEE DE JULIO ROMERO DE TORRES.
Installé dans le même bâtiment que le pré-
cédent, plaza del Potro.
Heures de visite: *Les mêmes que pour le
Musée Provincial des Beaux-Arts. Entrée
gratuite.*
MUSEE ARCHEOLOGIQUE PROVINCIAL.
Heures de visite: *Matin (toute l'année): de
10h à 13h 30. Après-midi (fermé en juillet
et en août, tous les dimanches et jours fériés
de l'année): janvier à avril et septembre à
décembre, de 16h à 18h; mai et juin, de 17h
à 19h. Prix de l'entrée: 20 pesetas.*
*MUSEE MUNICIPAL TAURIN ET DES ARTS
TYPIQUES.*
Heures de visite: *Matin (toute l'année): de
9h 30 à 13h 30. Après-midi du 1er mai au 30
septembre, de 17h à 20h; du 1er octobre au
30 avril, de 16h à 19h. Prix de l'entrée: 5
pesetas.*
PONT ROMAIN.
MURAILLES.
TOUR DE LA CALAHORRA. Construction
arabe, située à côté du pont romain, sur la
rive gauche du Guadalquivir.
Heures de visite: *Matin (toute l'année): de
9h 30 à 13h 30. Après-midi: du 1er mai au*

*30 septembre, de 17h à 20h; du 1er octobre
au 30 avril, de 16h à 19h. Prix de l'entrée;
5 pesetas.*
TOUR DE MALMUERTA.
PORTE DU PONT.
ALCAZAR DES ROIS CHRETIENS.
Heures de visite: *Matin (toute l'année): de
9h 30 à 13h 30; Après-midi: du 1er mai au
30 septembre, de 17h à 20h; du 1er octobre au
30 avril, de 16h à 19h; jardins illuminés,
du 1er mai au 30 septiembre, de 22h à 1h.
Prix de l'entrée: 10 pesetas; usage d'appa-
reils photographiques: 10 pesetas; visite des
jardins illuminés: 5 pesetas.*
SINAGOGUE.
CHAPELLE DE SAN BARTOLOME.
*EGLISE DE SANTA MARINA DE AGUAS
SANTAS.*
EGLISE DE SAN MIGUEL.
EGLISE CONVETUELLE DE SAN PABLO.
EGLISE DE SAN NICOLAS.
EGLISE DE SAN LORENZO.
EGLISE DE LA MAGDALENA.
COLLEGE DE LA COMPAGNIE.
PALAIS DE LA DEPUTATION.
MAISON DE L'INDIANO.
PALAIS DES MARQUIS DE VIANA.
PALAIS DES MARQUIS DE CARPIO.
MAISON DES VILLALONES.
CALLEJA DE LAS FLORES.
PLAZA DE LOS DOLORES.
MONUMENT AU TORERO «MANOLETE».
ZOCO. Dans la maison anciennement appelée
de «Las Bulas», bâtiment du XVIème siècle.
Marché de produits artisanaux. Entrée par
les rues de Judíos et d'Averroes.
AUBERGE DU POTRO.
PLAZA DE LA CORREDERA.
PATIOS. L'un des charmes de plus grand
intérêt qu'ait conservé Cordoue est consti-
tué par les «patios» de ses vieilles maisons.
Ceux des maisons seigneuriales et ceux des
maisons les plus humbles et les plus populai-
res rivalisent de cachet et de beauté.
MOULINS ARABES. En aval du pont romain
subsistent quelques moulins, parmi lesquels
les plus importants sont ceux de la Albaleña,
celui de l'Enmedio et le Moulin de Papier.
LES ERMITAGES. A 10 kilomètres de la capitale.
*MONASTERE DE SAN JERONIMO DE VAL-
PARAISO.* Dans les faubourgs de la capitale
et près de Medina Azahara.
RUINES DE MEDINA AZAHARA. Situées à
quelques kilomètres de la capitale.
Heures de visite: *Matin (toute l'année): de
9h 30 à 13h 30. Après-midi: du 16 mars au
15 septembre, de 16h à 19h 30; du 16 septembre au 15 mars, de 15h à 17h 30. Prix
de l'entrée: 15 pesetas.*

MONUMENTS

CATHEDRAL-MOSQUE. *Hours open to the
public: Mornings (all year) from 10.30 a.m.
to 1.30 p.m. Afternoons: January, February,*

November and December, from 3.30 p.m. to 5.30 p.m.; March and October, from 3.30 p.m. to 6.00 p.m.; April from 3.30 p.m. to 7.00 p.m.; May and August from 4.00 p.m. to 7.30 p.m.; September from 4.00 p.m. to 7.00 p.m.; June and July from 4.00 p.m. to 8.00 p.m. The hours for public worship are excluded from tourist hours. Entrance fee: 20 pesetas; children, 10 pesetas; camaras, 10 pesetas.

PROVINCIAL MUSEUM OF FINE ARTS.
Hours open to the public: Mornings: January to June and September to December, from 10.00 a.m. to 1.30 p.m.; July and August, all Sundays and fest days during the year, from 10.00 a.m. to 2.00 p.m. Afternoons: January, November and December, from 3.30 p.m. to 6.00 p.m.; April, May, June and September from 4.00 p.m. to 7.00 p.m. During July and August the Museum is closed every afternoon and for the whole day on the following dates: lst January, 24th October, 25th December and Good Friday. Entrance fee: 5 pesetas; Sundays, free of charge.

JULIO ROMERO DE TORRES MUSEUM. This is within the same building as the previous Museum, in the Plaza del Potro.
Hours open to the public: Same as the Provincial Museum of Fine Arts. Entrance free of charge.

PROVINCIAL ARCHEOLOGICAL MUSEUM.
Hours open to the public: Mornings (all the year): from 10.00 a.m. to 1.30 p.m. Afternoons (closed during July and August, all Sundays and festa days): January to April and September to December, from 4.00 p.m. to 6.00 p.m.; May and June, from 5.00 p.m. to 7.00 p.m. Entrance fee: 20 pesetas.

MUNICIPAL MUSEUM OF TAURINE AND TYPICAL ARTS.
Hours open to the public: Mornings (all the year) from 9.30 a.m. to 1.30 p.m. Afternoons from lst May to 30th September, from 5.00 p.m. to 8.00 p.m.; from lst October to 30th April, from 4.00 p.m. to 7.00 p.m. Entrance fee: 5 pesetas.

ROMAN BRIDGE.
RAMPARTS.
THE CALAHORRA TOWER. Of Arab construction, it stands next to the Roman Brigde on the left bank of the Guadalquivir River.
Open to the public: Mornings (all the year): from 9.30 to 1.30 p.m. Afternoons: from ist May to 30th September, from 5.00 p.m. to 8.00 p.m.; from lst October to 30th April, from 4.00 p.m. to 7.00 p.m. Entrance fee: 5 pesetas.

THE MALMUERTA TOWER.
THE GATEWAY TO THE BRIDGE.
THE FORTRESS OF THE CHRISTIAN KINGS.
Open to the public: Mornings (all the year): from 9.30 a.m. to 1.30 p.m. Afternoons: from lst May to 30th September, from 5.00 p.m. to 8.00 p.m.; from lst October to 30th April, from 4.00 p.m. to 7.00 p.m.; The lighted gardens from lst May to 30th September, from 10.00 p.m. to 1.00 a.m. Entrance fee: 10 pesetas; camaras 10 pesetas; lighted gardens 5 pesetas.

SYNAGOGUE.
SAINT BARTHOLOMEW'S CHAPEL.
CHURCH OF SAINT MARINA OF THE HOLY WATERS.
ST. MICHAEL'S CHURCH.
ST. PAUL'S CONVENT CHURCH.
ST. NICHOLAS' CHURCH.
ST. LAURENCE'S CHURCH.
CHURCH OF THE MAGDALENA.
SCHOOL OF THE COMPANIA
PALACE OF PROVINCIAL COUNCIL.
HOUSE OF THE INDIAN
PALACE OF THE MARQUIS OF VIANA.
PALACE OF THE MARQUIS OF CARPIO.
HOUSE OF THE VILLALONES.
THE LANE OF FLOWERS.
THE SQUARE OF GRIEF.
MONUMENT TO MANOLETE.
ZOCO. In the house which was called in olden days «Las Bulas», a building belonging to the 16th century. Market of handicraft work. Entrances given on to the Judios Street and the Averroes Street.
INN OF THE FOAL.
SQUARE OF THE CORREDERA.
COURTYARDS. The courtyards in the old houses are one of the most interesting attractions in Córdoba. Whether in manors or in the most humble and poor houses, they all compete in beauty and taste.
ARAB MILLS. Several mills have been preserved down river from the Roman Bridge, among which the Albolafia Mill, the Enmedio Mill and the Paper Mill are the most outstanding.
THE HERMITAGES. These are 10 kilometres from the capital.
MONASTERY OF SAN JERONIMO DE VALPARAISO. On the outskirts of the capital near Medina Azahara.
MEDINA AZAHARA RUINS. A few kilometres from the capital.
Hours open to the public: Mornings (all the year): 9.30 a.m. to 1.30 p.m. Afternoons: from 16th March to 15th September, from 4.00 p.m. to 7.30 p.m.; 16 September to 15 March from 3.00 p.m. to 5.30 p.m. Entrance fee: 15 pesetas.

BAUWERKE

MEZQUITA - KATHEDRALE. Besichtigung: morgens von 10,30 bis 13.30 (ganz-jährig); Nachmittags: Januar, Februar, November und Dezember von 15,30 bis 17.30; März und Oktober von 15.30 bis 18.00; April von 15.30 bis 19.00; Mai und August von 15.30 bis 19.00; September von 16.00 bis 19.00; Juni und Juli von 16.00 bis 20.00; Besichtigungen während der Messe gestattet.

Eintritt: 20 pts., Kinder 10 pts., Fotografieren 10 pts.

MUSEUM DER SCHÖNEN KÜNSTE. Besichtigungen: morgens von Januar bis Juni und von September bis Dezember von 10.00 bis 13.30. Juli und August und an allen Sonn— und Feiertagen von 10.00 bis 14.00; nachmittags: Januar, November und Dezember von 15.30 bis 17.30; März und Oktober von 15.30 bis 18.00; April, Mai, Juni und September von 16.00 bis 19.00. Im Juli und August nachmittags und am 1. Januar, 24. Oktober, 25. Dezember und Karfreitag ganztägig geschlossen. Eintrittspreis: 5 pts, sonntags gratis.

MUSEUM JULIO ROMERO DE TORRES. Im gleichen Gebäude wie das Museum der Schönen Künste, auf der Plaza del Potro. Besichtigungszeiten: siehe oben. Eintritt frei.

ARCHÄOLOGISCHES MUSEUM. Besichtigungen: morgens (ganzjährig) von 10.00 bis 13.30 nachmittags: (Juli und August ebenso wie an Sonn-und Feiertagen geschlossen); von Januar bis April und von September bis Dezember von 16.00 bis 18.00; Mai und Juni von 17.00 bis 19.00. Eintritt: 20 pts.

MUSEUM FÜR STIERKAMPF UND FOLKLORE. Besichtigung: morgens (ganzjährig) von 9.30 bis 13.30. Nachmittags: vom 1. Mai bis 30. September von 17.00 bis 20.00; vom 1. Oktober bis 30. April von 16.00 bis 19.00. Eintritt: 5 pts.

RÖMISCHE BRÜCKE.
BEFESTIGUNGSMAUERN.
TURM DER CALAHORRA. Arabisches Bauwerk in der Nähe der Römischen Brücke, links des Guadalquivir. Besichtigungen: morgens (ganzjährig) von 9.30 bis 13.30. Nachmittags: vom 1. Mai bis 30. September von 17.00 bis 20.00 vom 1. Oktober bis 30. April von 16.00 bis 19.00. Eintritt: 5 pts.
TURM DEL MALMUERTA.
PUERTA DEL PUENTE.
ALCAZAR DE LOS REYES CRISTIANOS. Besichtigung: morgens (ganzjährig) von 9.30 bis 13.30. Nachmittags: von 1. Mai bis 30. September von 17.00 bis 20.00; vom 1. Oktober bis 30 April von 16.00 bis 19.00; die erleuchtetem gärten vom 1. Mai bis 30. September von 22.00 bis 1.00. Eintritt: 10 pts., Fotografieren 10 pts., Besuch der beleuchteten Gärten, 5 pts.
SYNAGOGE.
KAPELLE SAN BARTOLOMÉ.
KIRCHE SANTA MARINA DE AGUAS SANTAS.
KIRCHE SAN MIGUEL.
KLOSTERKIRCHE SAN PABLO.
KIRCHE SAN NICOLÁS.
KIRCHE SAN LORENZO.
MAGDALENENKIRCHE.
COLEGIO DE LA COMPAÑIA.

RATSHAUS.
CASA DEL INDIANO.
PALAIS DES MARQUES DE VIANA.
PALAIS DES MARQUES DEL CARPIO.
HAUS DER VILLALONES.
CALLEJA DE LAS FLORES.
PLAZA DE LOS DOLORES.
DENKMAL MANOLETES.
ZOCO. Kunsthandwerkbazar, in dem früher «Las Bulas» benannten Haus, einem Gebäude des 16. Jahrhunderts. Eingang durch die Calle de Judíos und die Calle Averroes.
GASTHOF «EL POTRO».
PLAZA DE LA CORREDERA.
INNENHÖFE. Eine der reizvollsten und interessantesten Sehenswürdigkeiten Córdobas sind die innenhöfe ihrer alten Häuser. Herrenhäuser und die Häuser der ärmstens sind sich gleich an Schönheit und Geschmack.
MAURISCHE MÜHLEN. Flußabwärts der Römischen Brücke sind noch verschiedene Mühlen erhalten, unter denen besonders die Albolafia, die von Enmedio und die Papiermühle hervorstechen.
DIE EINSIEDELEI, 10 km von der Hauptstadt entfernt.
DAS KLOSTER SAN JERONIMO DE VALPARAISO, am Stadtrand, in der Nähe von Medina Azahara.
DIE RUINEN VON MEDINA AZAHARA, einige wenige Kilometer von der Hauptstadt entfernt. Besichtigung: morgerns (ganzjährig) von 9.30 bis 13.30. Nachmittags: vom 16. März bis 15. September von 16.00 bis 19.30 vom 16. September bis 15. März von 15.00 bis 17.30. Eintritt: 15 pts.

HOTELES
HÔTELS
HOTELS
HOTELS
Córdoba

PARADOR NACIONAL DE LA ARRUZAFA. Avda. de la Arruzafa, s/n. Telf. 22 62 40. H * * * *

GRAN CAPITAN. Avda. América, 3 y 5. Teléf. 22 19 55. H * * * *

MELIA-CORDOBA. Jardines de la Victoria. Teléf. 22 63 80. H * * * *

EL CORDOBES. Avda. de Medina Azahara, 7. Teléf. 23 16 36. H * * *

ZAHIRA. Conde Robledo, 1. Teléf. 22 62 60. H * * *

MARISA. Cardenal Herrero, 6. Teléf. 22 63 17. HR * *

SELU. Eduardo Dato, 7. Teléfono 22 38 65. HR * *

SIMON. Avda. del Gran Capitán, 5. Telf. 22 19 19. H * *

ANDALUCIA. José Zorrilla, 3. Telf. 22 18 55. HR *

AVENIDA. Avda. del Generalísimo, 26. Telf. 22 39 00. HR *
GRANADA. Avda. de América, 21. Telf. 22 18 63. H *
NIZA. Plaza de Aladreros, 7. H *
SERRANO. Pérez Galdós, 4. Telf. 22 62 98 HR *
LUIS DE GONGORA. Horno de la Trinidad, 7. Telf. 22 19 67. HR * * *
ALHAKEN. Alhaken II, 6. Telf. 22 15 93. HR * *
EL BRILLANTE. Avda. del Brillante, 91. Telf. 22 62 40 H * *
CUATRO NACIONES. García Morato, 4. Telf. 22 39 25. H * *
MERIDIONAL. Ramírez de Arellano, 8. Telf. 22 19 31. HR * *
MEZQUITA. Rogelio Vignote, 2. Telf. 22 22 20. HR *
MONTES. Avda. América, 25. Telf. 22 38 51. H * *
SANTA MARINA. Isabel Losa, 10. Telf. 22 59 84. HR * *
ARCANGEL. Velázquez Bosco, 13. Telf. 22 48 47. H *
COMERCIAL. Moreira, 7. Telf. 22 37 88. HR *
LA IDEAL. Fitero, 5. Telf. 22 29 94. HR *
EL LEON. Céspedes, 12. Telf. 22 30 21. HR *
MUÑOZ. Duque de Fernán Núñez, 2. Telf. 22 61 23. HR *
PERALES. Avda. Mozárabe, 13 dup. Telf. 23 21 12. HR *
EL QUINI. Ctra. Madrid-Cádiz. Km. 413. H *
ROMA. Juan de Mena, 4. Telf. 22 56 93. HR *
SENECA. Conde y Luque, 7. HR *
ULIA. Victoriano Rivera, 4. Telf. 22 57 37. HR *

Aguilar de la Frontera

LAS VIÑAS. Ctra. Córdoba-Málaga. Km. 455. Telf. 375. H * *

Baena

IPONUBA. Nicolás Alcalá, 7. Telf. 54. H * *

Belmez

PLAYA. Finca Abubillo. Telf. 109. H *

Cabra

PALLARES. Alcalde Galiano, 2. Telf. 434. HR * *

Lucena

BALTANAS. Avda. José Solís, s/n. Telf. 221. HR * *
BILILA. Plaza del Generalísimo, 21. Telf. 55. H *

Montilla

FELIPE. San Francisco, 27. Telf. 27. H *

Priego de Córdoba

RAFI. Isabel la Católica, 4. HR *
XANIA. José Antonio, 9. Telf. 348. H *

Puente Genil

RUCE. Susana Benítez, 50. Telf. 636. H *

Villaharta

BALNEARIO. Ctra. Badajoz-Granada. Km. 235. HR *

ACAMPAMENTOS TURISTICOS
CAMPINGS
TOURIST CAMPS
ZELTPLÄTZE

CAMPAMENTO MUNICIPAL DE TURISMO. Ctra. Córdoba-Villaviciosa Km. 2. Telf. 22 62 40 (708) 1.ª C.
CERCA DE LAGARTIJO. Ctra. Madrid-Cádiz. Km 398. Telf. 25 04 26. 1.ª C.

RESTAURANTES
RESTAURANTS
RESTAURANTS
RESTAURANTS

EL ZOCO. Calle Judíos, s/n.
EL BOSQUE. Avda. del Brillante, 122.
CASTILLO DE LA ALBAIDA. Ctra. La Albaida, Km 4.
LA TORRECILLA. Ctra. Sevilla, Km. 406.
ANDALUCIA. José Zorrilla, 3
EL CABALLO ROJO. Deanes, 8.
LOS CALIFAS. Deanes, 9.
CAMPING MUNICIPAL. Ctra. Brillante.
EL CARMEN. Avda. Jesús Rescatado, 15.
CERCA DE LAGARTIJO. Ctra. Madrid-Cádiz. Km. 398.
COSTA SOL. Glorieta Gral. Moscardó.
DOS AVENIDAS. Avda. América, 33.
FULVIO'S. José María Herrero, 7.
GRAN BAR. Plaza de José Antonio, 1.
LA HOSTELERIA. Sevilla, 2.
IMPERIO. Victoriano Rivera, 6.
IVORY. Marqués Boil, 5.
LARREA. Avda. Jesús Rescatado, 15.
MERCANTIL. Morería, 19.
MERENDERO LOS CALIFAS. Saldaña, s/n.
MESON DEL CONDE. Medina y Cornella, s/n.
MESON LA JUDERIA. Judería, 13.
EL MOLINO ROJO. Jardines de la Victoria, s/n.
MOYA. Ctra. Madrid, Km. 400.
PLATA. Julio Pellicer, 22.
POSADA DEL MAR. Avda. de Cádiz, 79.
LA PRIMERA. Ctra. del Brillante, 26.
RENAULT. Avda. América, 3 y 5.

REPOSTERIA CIRCULO DE LABRADORES.
José Zorrilla, s/n.
SALAMANCA. Victoriano Rivera, 8.
SAN CARLOS. Ctra. Madrid, Km. 399.
SAVARIN. Avda. Generalísimo, s/n.
VALENCIA. Ctra. Madrid, 105.
LA VERDAD. Morería, 13.
BALSERA. Avda. República Argentina, 10.
EL BARRIL. Fernández Grilo, 5.
CALIFORNIA. Ctra. Madrid-Cádiz, Km. 405.
FORD. Ctra. Madrid, Km. 398.
MADRID. Ctra. Madrid, 99.
MARIANO. Avda. Cádiz, 60.
MATIAS. Ctra. Palma del Río, Km. 7.
ROSALES. Avda. Generalísimo, s/n.

Alcolea

CARMONA. Ctra., 72.
LAS VEGAS. Ctra. Madrid-Cádiz, Km. 388.
CENTRAL. Carretera, 4.
CORDOBA. Carretera, 10.

Baena

IPONUBA. Nicolás Alcalá, 7.
CAPITOL. Plaza Sáenz de Buruaga, 14.
LOS CLAVELES. Sanjurjo, 6.
FLORIDA. General Sanjurjo, 11.
PISCINA. Ctra. Badajoz-Granada, Km, 338.
SABRINA. Sáenz de Buruaga, 12.

Belmez

DOMINGUEZ. Ctra. Badajoz-Granada, s/n.

Bujalance

SIETE PUERTAS. Mártires, 1.

Cabra

FERYLA. Alcalá Galiano, 2.
FUENTE DEL RIO. Parque de la Fuente del Río.

La Carlota

EL JARDIN. Ctra. Madrid-Cádiz, Km. 433.

El Carpio

EL QUINI. Ctra. Madrid-Cádiz, Km. 25.

Castro del Río

POSTAS LA PARADA. Ctra. Badajoz-Granada, Km. 317.

Cerro Muriano

LOS PINARES. Ctra. Córdoba-Badajoz, Km. 15,500.
EL FRENAZO. Ctra. Almadén, Km. 11.
GRAN PARADA. Ctra. Almadén, Km. 10,800.
X. Carretera, 25.

Encinas Reales

VILLA GRACIA. Arrecife, 2.

Espejo

CASA LORENZO. Regiones Devastadas, 6.

Fernán-Núñez

MOLERO. Ctra. Córdoba-Málaga, 3.

Fuente Obejuna

MATADERO FRIGORIFICO. Paseo de José Antonio, s/n.

Lucena

BILILA HIJO. Avda. José Solís, s/n.
COGOLLO. Calvo Sotelo, 108.

Montilla

LAS CAMACHAS. Ctra. Málaga, Km. 466.
LOS ARCOS. Plaza José Antonio, 1.

Montoro

ANDALUCIA. Ctra. Madrid-Cádiz, Km, 357,6.
BELSAY. Rosario, 2.
CLUB CAÑERO. Plaza de José Antonio, 2.

Monturque

LOS FAROLES. Carretera Madrid-Málaga, Km. 463.

Peñarroya-Pueblonuevo

EL CORTIJO. Calvo Sotelo, 52.
LA PISCINA. Carretera Badajoz-Granada, Km. 192.
SAN ANTONIO. Sol, 9.

Pozoblanco

LA PONDEROSA. Cronista Sepúlveda, 8.

Priego de Córdoba

LOS MARISCOS. Torrejón, 7.
RAFI. Plaza San Pedro, 4.

Puente Genil

CENTRAL. Francisco Domínguez, 2.
LAS VEGAS. Susana Benítez, 52.

Quintana

EL NOVENTA. Quintana, s/n.

Villafanca de Córdoba

LA HERRADURA. Carretera Madrid-Cádiz,
Km. 376.

Villarrubia

ESTACION DE SERVICIO. Ctra. Palma del
Río, Km. 12,3.

ESPECIALIDADES GASTRONOMICAS

La cocina cordobesa presenta atrayentes pla-
tos. Entre los más típicos figuran el cordero
a la caldereta, el estofado de rabos de toro,
el cochifrito, las manos de cerdo a la cordobesa, las ancas de rana con tomate, los
huevos «a como salgan», los espárragos
trigueros o silvestres en cazuela, el fresco
salmorejo y el clásico gazpacho de tomate,
de haba o de almendra.

Cuenta con postres propios, tales como la
carne de membrillo y jalea de Puente Genil y
los «alfajores» de Montilla (ambos productos
calificados «los mejores del mundo» en
certámenes internacionales), los anisados
de Rute, las compotas de membrillo (de
confección doméstica), las granadas de
Castro del Río, las naranjas de Palma, el
pastel cordobés de hojaldre y sidra y, final-
mente, la popular «sangria», compuesta por
vino tinto, gaseosa, frutas picadas, canela
en rama y azúcar.

Vinos

Son universalmente famosos los vinos de
Montilla y Moriles, denominación de origen
protegida por el Estado. Por su finura única
se encuentran incluidos entre los mejores
de nuestra Patria.

Estos vinos se producen en una extensa co-
marca sobre la que podemos trazar, entre
varias, una ruta ideal del vino, que, partiendo
de Córdoba capital, recorriera las localidades
de Montilla, Aguilar de la Frontera, Moriles,
Puente Genil, Cabra, Lucena, Fernán Núñez,
Montemayor y Monturque, con visitas a la-
gares, bodegas y centros de degustación, en
los que el visitante puede conocer las
excelencias de estos vinos.

SPECIALITES GASTRONOMIQUES

*La cuisine cordouane présente des plats
délicieux. Parmi les plus typiques figurent
l'agneau en ragoût («a la caldereta»), les
queues de taureau à l'étouffée, le ragoût de
chevreau («cochifrito»), les pieds de porc à
la cordouane, les cuisses de grenouille à
la tomate, les oeufs «au petit bonheur,
les asperges sauvages en ragoût, le frais
saupiquet, et le classique «gazpacho» à la
tomate, aux fèves ou aux amandes.*

Elle a ses desserts propres tels que la gelée

*et la confiture de coings de Puente Genil
les gâteaux au miel de Montilla (deux
produits reconnus comme «les meilleurs du
monde» dans des concours internationaux),
les anisettes de Rute, les compotes de
coings (de confection domestique), les
grenades de Castro del Río, les oranges de
Palma, le gâteau feuilleté cordouan au
cidre, et, finalement, la populaire «sangria»,
composée de vin rouge, de limonade, de
fruits hâchés, de canelle en branche et de
sucre.*

Vins

*Les vins de Montilla et de Moriles, appellation
d'origine protégée par l'Etat, sont universelle-
ment connus. Grâce à leur finesse unique,
ils sont inclus parmi les meilleurs de notre
Patrie.*

*Ces vins sont produits dans une vaste région,
dans laquelle on peut tracer, parmi plusieurs, une route du vin idéale, qui, partant de
Cordoue, passe par les villes de Montilla,
Aguilar de la Frontera, Moriles, Puente Genil,
Cabra, Lucena, Fernán Núñez, Montemayor
et Monturque, avec des visites aux pressoirs,
aux caves et aux centres de dégustation,
dans lesquels le visiteur peut apprécier les
qualités de ces vins.*

CULINARY SPECIALITIES

Typical Cordovan food is made up of very
attractive dishes, the most typical of which
are the lamb stew, bull-tail stew, fricasse
of lamb, pigs feet a la Cordobesa, frog's
rump with tomato, eggs «anyhow», wi-ld
esparagus stewed, fresh salmorejo sauce
and the classical Gazpacho of tomato,
broad beans or almonds.

It also has typical sweets such as quince meat,
Puente Genil jelly, the Montilla almond and
honey pastes (both products have been
qualified as the «best in the world» in inter-
national competitions), the Rute anisettes,
home-made quince jam, the Castro del Río
pomegranates, the oranges from Palma,
the Cordovan cake of puff pastry and cider
and lastly the popular «sangria» mad of
red wine, lemonade, diced fruit, cinnamon
and sugar.

Wines

The wines from Montilla and Moriles, called
after their place of origen and given State
protection, are world famous. They are
included among Spain's best wines for
their unique delicate flavour.

These wines are produced over a wide area.
A «wine» route, the ideal one among several,
could be drawn up, starting from Córdoba,
the capital, passing through Montilla, Aguilar de la Frontera, Moriles, Puente Genil,

Cabra, Lucena, Fernán Núñez, Montemayor and Monturque, including visits to wine cellars and bars where the visitor can get to know these excellent wines.

GASTRONOMISCHE SPEZIALITÄTEN

Die kordobesische Küche bietet viele apetitanregende Gerichte. Spezialitäten sind unter anderem: Lammbraten a la caldereta, Ochsenschwanzbraten, gebratenes Ferkel, Schweinehacksen a la Cordobesa, Froschschenkel mit Tomate, Eier «a como salgam», junger grüner Spargel a la cazuela, die Sauce «salmoreja», und der traditionelle Gazpacho aus Tomaten, Bohnen oder Mandeln.

Auch auf dem Gebiet des Nachtischs gibt es Spezialitäten: Quittengelee, und Quittenmus aus Puente Genil und die Gewürzkuchen aus Montilla (beides von Weltrang), Anisbranntweine aus Rute, der hausgemachte Quittenkompott, die Granatäpfer aus Castro del Río, die Orangen aus Palma, das Kordobesische Gebäck aus Blatterteig und Apfelwein, und schließlich die berühmte Sangría, die aus Rotwein, Sprudel, Obststückchen, Zimtstangen und Zucker.

Weine

Die Weine aus Montilla und Moriles sind weltbekannt, und ihr Name ist als Markenbezeichnung staatlich geschützt. Ihres einzigartig feinen Geschmacks wegen zählt man sie zu den besten Weinen Spaniens. Diese Weine werden auf einem großen Terrain angebaut, durch das man eine ideale Weinstraße ziehen kann, die von der Stadt Córdoba aus über Montilla, Aguilar de la Frontera, Moriles, Puente Genil, Cabra, Lucena, Fernán Núñez und Montemayor nach Monturque führtm, mit Besuchen in Keltereien, Weinkellern und Probierstuben, wo der Besucher die ausgezeichnete Qualität dieser Weine kennenlernen kann.

CAFETERIAS Y BARES
CAFETERIAS ET BARS
CAFETERIAS AND BARS
CAFES UND BARS

MAGERIT. Eduardo Lucena, 2.
MILKO. Jesús María, 16.
RIVIERA. Cruz Conde, 17.
ROYAL. Cruz Conde, 3.
LAS VEGAS. Gondomar, 19.
GRAN CAPITAN. Avenida de América, 5 y 7.
MESON DE LA LUNA. Calleja de la Luna, s/n.
CASA PEPE. Romero, 1.
MESON LAGAR DE LA MEZQUITA. Avda. Viñuela.
BAVIERA. Pastores, 5.

EL HIDALGO. Plaza Carrillos.
EL PUERTO. Victoriano Rivera, s/n.
CRISMONA. Huelva, 17.
EL CORAL. Avda. de Cádiz. Sector Sur.
GRANADA. Avda. Granada, 9.
GUERRERO. Gran Capitán, 23.
LAS VEGAS. Gondomar, 19.
MOKA. G. Morato, 1.
NIZA. Gral. Moscardó, s/n.
PULVIO'S. José María Herrero, 7.
RENAULT. Avda. de América, 3 y 5.
OASIS. Avda. Cádiz, 405.
SAN ANTONIO. Pta. del Rincón, 24.
SAN CARLOS. Polig. Fuensanta, Bl. 6.
TURIN. Avda. Doctor Fleming, s/n.

LIBRERIAS
LIBRAIRIES
BOOK SHOPS
BUCHHANDLUNGN

AGORA. Avda. Antonio Maura, 43.
AIXA. García Morato, 4.
CANETE. Concepción, 2.
IBERICA. José Antonio, 1.
IDEAL. Cuesta Luján, 1.
VDA. DE LUQUE. Gondomar, 13.
VDA. DE RAFAEL MARIN. Realejo, 4.
SAN PELAGIO. Amador de los Ríos, 1.
SENECA. San Alvaro, 5.

CORREOS, TELEGRAFOS Y TELEFONOS
POSTES, TELEGRAPHES ET TELEPHONES
POST OFFICE, TELEGRAMS AND TELEPHONES
POSTÄMTER, TELEGRAMM UND TELEFONZENTRALEN

CORREOS. Cruz Conde, 21. Telf. 22 18 12.
TELEGRAFOS. Cruz Conde, 21. Telf. 22 26 05. Telebén 22 35 32.
TELEFONOS. Plaza de José Antonio, 7. Teléfonos: Información, 003; Interurbanas, 009.

CENTROS OFICIALES
CENTRES OFFICIELS
OFFICIAL CENTRES
OFFIZIELLE GEBÄUDE

OFICINA DE INFORMACION Y TURISMO. Avda. del Gran Capitán, 13. Telf. 22 12 05.
GOBIERNO CIVIL. Avda. del Gran Capitán, 18. Telf. 22 53 82.
DELEGACION PROVINCIAL DE INFORMACION Y TURISMO. Hermanos González Murga, 17. Telf. 22 10 54.
OFICINA MUNICIPAL DE TURISMO. Plaza de Judá Leví. Telf. 22 40 99.
SEGURO TURISTICO C.A.P. Avda. del Generalísimo, 25. Telf. 22 58 07.
COMISARIA DE POLICIA (Pasaportes). Avda. Dr. Fleming. Telf. 22 24 28.

JUZGADOS DE GUARDIA NUMS. 1 y 2. Sevilla, 2. Telfs. 22 41 66 y 22 28 10.
JUZGADOS DE GUARDIA NUMS. 3 y 4. Sevilla, 2. Telfs. 22 51 84 y 22 36 23.
PARQUE DE BOMBEROS. Ctra. Granja del Estado. Telf. 23 27 73.
CASA DE SOCORRO. Góngora. Telf. 22 29 10.
CRUZ ROJA ESPAÑOLA. Paseo de la Victoria, s/n. Telf. 22 38 73 y 22 38 20.
HOSPITAL PROVINCIAL. Ctra. Vecinal Alameda del Obispo. Telf. 23 42 00.
AMBULATORIO DEL SEGURO DE ENFERDAD. Avda. de América, 1. Telf. 22 23 82.
CASA DE MATERNIDAD. Residencia Infantil «Virgen del Carmen». Puerta Nueva. Telf. 25 04 50.
JEFATURA DE LA POLICIA MUNICIPAL. Campo Madre de Dios. Telf. 25 14 14 y 25 27 94.
SUBDIRECTOR DE TRAFICO DE LA GUARDIA CIVIL. Avda. Medina Azahara, 2. Telf. 23 37 53.

AGENCIAS DE VIAJE
AGENCES DE VOYAGES
TRAVEL AGENCIES
REISEBÜROS

VIAJES MELIA. Gondomar, 6. Telf. 22 42 69.
VIAJES ESPAÑA MUNDIAL. Puerta Osario, 2. Telf. 22 31 33.
VIAJES VINCIT. Alonso de Burgos, 7. Telf. 22 68 46.
VIAJES TORREMOLINOS. (American Express). Torrijos, 8. Telf. 22 74 84.
COMPAÑIA INTERNACIONAL DE COCHES CAMAS WAGONS-LIST/COOK. Cruz Conde, 28. Telf. 22 31 55.
VIAJES BONANZA. Avda. de Cervantes, 22. Telf. 22 67 21.
VIAJES NEVADA. Morería, s/n. Telf. 22 64 11.

COMUNICACIONES
COMMUNICATIONS
COMMUNICATIONS
VERKEHRSVERBINDUGEN

Ferrocarriles - Chemins de fer - Railways - Eisenbahn

RENFE (Oficina de Viajes). Venta anticipada de billetes. Avda. del Generalísimo, 10. Telf. 22 16 48.
ESTACION FERROCARRIL. Avda. de América. Telf. 22 29 88.
Servicios regulares con Madrid, Sevilla, Cádiz, Huelva, Málaga, Jaén, Granada, Algeciras, Valencia y Barcelona.

Líneas Aéreas - Lignes Aeriennes Airlines-Luftfahrtgesellschaften

IBERIA. Hotel Córdoba-Meliá. Paseo de la Victoria. Telf. 22 53 77. Servicios regulares con Madrid y Málaga.

AEROPUERTO NACIONAL DE CORDOBA. Finca Lavaderos. Telf. 23 23 00.

Autobuses - Autobus - Buses - Buslinien

Líneas regulares a:
VALENCIA. Agustín Moreno, 167 (Bar «El 6»). Telf. 25 11 08.
SEVILLA. Avda. del Gran Capitán, 12. Telf. 22 20 40.
GRANADA. Avda. del Gran Capitán, 12. Telf. 22 20 40.
JAEN. Avda. de América, 25. Telf. 22 17 74.
BADAJOZ. Avda. de América (Estación Ferrocarril). Telf. 22 29 88.

TAXIS
TAXIS
TAXIS
TAXIS

AVENIDA DE AMERICA. Telf. 22 32 64.
CARDENAL HERRERO. Telf. 22 51 42.
CAÑERO. (barriada) Telf. 25 19 95.
GRAN CAPITAN (primer tramo) Telf. 22 48 71.
GRAN CAPITAN (segundo tramo). Telf. 22 51 53.
GENERAL MOSCARDO (Ciudad Jardin). Telf. 23 20 42.
PLAZA DE JOSE ANTONIO. Telf. 22 36 76.
PUERTA OSARIO. Telf. 22 13 06.
UBEDA (sector sur). Telf. 23 20 43.
HOTEL CORDOBA-MELIA. Telf. 22 51 33.
RESIDENCIA SEGURO ENFERMEDAD. Telf. 23 20 41.

ALQUILER DE AUTOMOVILES
SIN CONDUCTOR
LOCATION D'AUTOS
SANS CHAUFFEUR
CAR-HIRE WITHOUT ADRIVER
AUTOVERMIETUNG OHNE FAHRER

DON JUAN F. GARRIDO PEREZ. José M.ª Herrero, 22. Telf. 23 28 06.
DON MIGUEL MARQUEZ SANCHEZ. Marqués del Boil, 3. Telf. 42 71 33.
AUTOMOVILES GARCIA. Felipe II, 1. Telf. 23 37 60.
DON BARTOLOME GARRIDO MOHEDANO. José M.ª Herrero, 22.
DON JUAN JOSE A. SANTIAGO FERNANDEZ. Avda. de América, 53. Telf. 23 24 32.
DON LUIS CABEZA CABEZA. Paseo del General Primo de Rivera, 33. Telf. 22 13 75.
AUTO RUTA. Doce de Octubre, 19. Telf. 22 57 42.
HERTZ DE ESPAÑA S. A. Torrijos, 8. Telf. 22 74 84.
VIAJES VINCIT. Alonso de Burgos, 7. Telf. 22 68 46.
AUTOCAR. Antonio Maura, 3. Telf. 23 20 11.

TALLERES DE REPARACION
DE AUTOMOVILES
ATELIERS DE REPARATION
D'AUTOMOVILES
CAR REPAIR GARAGES
AUTOREPARATUR-WERKSTÄTTEN

TALLERES COSTAN. Diego Serrano, 21. Telf. 21 13 18.
TALLERES COOPERATIVA AUTOMOVILISTA. Ctra. de Sevilla, Km. 405. Telf. 23 15 00.
TALLERES MECANICOS GEMASA. Ctra. de Sevilla. Km. 405. Telf. 23 57 00.
SERVICIO OFICIAL CITROEN. Diego Serrano, 12. Telf. 23 25 15.
SERVICIO OFICIAL PEGASO. Ctra. de Sevilla, Km. 405,5. Telf. 23 41 96.
SERVICIO OFICIAL BARREIROS. Avda. de Cádiz, s/n. Telf. 23 41 03.
SERVICIO RENAULT. Avda. de América, 3 y 5. Telf. 22 38 93.
SERVICIO SEAT. José M.ª Herrero, 7. Telf. 23 33 00.
AUTORREPARACION DARIO. Julio Pellicer, 2. Telf. 23 13 58.
ROTINI Y CIA. Avda. de Cádiz, 52. Telf. 23 26 78.
TALLER ETYCA. Avda. de los Almogávares. Telf. 25 08 84.
TALLERES VOLKSWAGEN. Ctra. de Madrid, 85. Telf. 25 14 82.
SERVICIO OFICIAL MORRIS-MG. Avda. de Cádiz, 58. Telf. 23 23 01.

GARAJES
GARAGE
GARAGE
GARAGE

IMPERIAL. Obispo Mardones, s/n.
CORDOBA. Ctra. de Sevilla, Km. 405.
VILCHEZ. Avda. de Jesús Rescatado, 42.
SUR. Avda. de Cádiz, 50-A.
ARCE. Capitán Cortés, 10.
SAN JOSE. Plaza de Colón, 34.
ESPAÑA. Plaza de España, s/n.
PALACE. Miguel Benzo, s/n.
CERVANTES. Avda. de Cervantes, 14.
CIUDAD JARDIN. José M.ª Herrero, 22.
SAN CAYETANO. Avda. Obispo Pérez Muñoz, 14.
AUTOCAR. Antonio Maura, 3.
ALCAZAR. Dr. Fleming, 1.
AMERICA. Avda. de América, 17.
VICTORIA. Gran Capitán, 23.
ARCANGEL. Los Alderetes, 5 y 7.
DAMASCO. La previsión, s/n.
RENAULT. Avda. de América, 3 y 5.
REYES CATOLICOS. Reyes Católicos, 24.

ESTACIONES DE SERVICIO
POSTE D'ESENCE
SERVICE STATIONS
TANKSTELLEN

CORDOBA. Plaza de Colón.

CORDOBA. Ctra. Madrid-Cádiz, Km. 405.
CORDOBA. Avda. República Argentina.
CORDOBA. Ctra. Madrid-Cádiz, Km. 404,8.
CORDOBA. Ctra. Madrid-Cádiz, Km. 400,5.
CORDOBA. Ctra. Madrid-Cádiz, Km. 398,8.
AGUILAR DE LA FRONTERA. Ctra. Córdoba Málaga, Km. 455,7.
ALCOLEA. Ctra. Madrid-Cádiz, Km. 388,1.
BAENA. Ctra. Badajoz-Granada, Km. 338,7.
BUJALANCE. Ctra. Córdoba-Almería, Km. 43,1.
EL CARPIO. Ctra. Madrid-Cádiz, Km. 373,2.
LUCENA. Ctra. Cuesta Espino-Málaga, Km. 56,2.
LUCENA. Ctra. Cuesta Espino-Málaga, Km. 55.
MONTILLA. Ctra. Córdoba-Málaga, Km. 27,5.
MONTORO. Ctra. Madrid-Cádiz, Km. 358,7.
PALMA DEL RIO. Ctra. Madrid-Cádiz.
POSADAS. Ctra. Córdoba-Palma del Río, Km. 32,5.
POZOBLANCO. Ctra. Andújar-Villanueva del Duque. Km. 94,4.
PRIEGO DE CORDOBA. Cruce Ctra. Alcalá la Real-Priego.
LA VICTORIA. Ctra. Madrid-Cádiz. Km. 425,9.
VILLANUEVA DE CORDOBA. Ctra. Villanueva Serena-Andújar, Km. 71,7.
VILLARRUBIA. Ctra. Córdoba-Palma del Río. Km. 12,3.

TEATROS Y CINES
THEATRES ET CINE
THEATRES AND CINEMAS
THEATER UND KINOS

GRAN TEATRO. Avda. del Gran Capitán, 3.
ALCAZAR. Reyes Católicos, 15.
ISABEL LA CATOLICA. Puerta del Rincón.
PALACIO DEL CINE. Plaza de José Antonio, sin número.
GONGORA. Jesús María, 12.
LUCANO. Calle Lucano.
DUQUE DE RIVAS. Avda. del Gran Capitán, 14.
CABRERA. Julio Pellicer, s/n.
CORDOBA. Ubeda, 2.
SENECA. Obispo Rojas Sandoval, 1.
OSIO. Joaquín Benjumea.
MAGDALENA. Plaza de la Magdalena, 2.
SANTA ROSA. Cruz de Juárez.
IRIS. Ruano Girón, 29.

SALAS DE FIESTAS
CABARETS
NIGHT CLUBS
TANZLOKALE

AZAHARA. Plaza de Judá Leví.
AMBAR. Paseo de la Victoria, 15.
GOLDEN CLUB (discoteca). Eduardo Quero, 3.
SAINT CYR (discoteca). Cruz Conde, 17.
RIO CLUB (discoteca). Avda. de Granada, 5.

TABLAOS FLAMENCOS
SPECTACLES FLAMENCOS
FLAMENCO SHOWS
FLAMENCOVORSTELLUNGEN

EL ZOCO. (Sito en el Museo Municipal Taurino y de Arte Cordobés).

PLAZA DE TOROS
ARENES
BULLRINGS
STIERKAMPFARENAS

Corridas de toros sobre el 25 de mayo. Avda. Parque.

CLUBS Y SOCIEDADES DEPORTIVAS
CLUBS ET SOCIETES SPORTIVES
CLUBS AND SPORTS CLUBS
CLUBS UND SPORTCLUBS

GRUPO DE CAZA DE EDUCACION Y DES-CANSO. Avda. del Gran Capitán, 10.
SOCIEDAD DE CAZADORES. Cruz Conde, 3.
CLUB GUADIATO. Doce de Octubre, 1.
CLUB CIUDAD JARDIN. José M.ª Valdenebro, 10.
CLUB SAN RAFAEL. Sta. M.ª de Gracia, 7.
SOCIEDAD DE PESCA FRAY ALBINO. Salvador Salido, 15.

PISCINAS
PISCINES
SWIMMING POOLS
SCHWIMMBÄDER

PISCINA MUNICIPAL. Avda. del Brillante.
PISCINA FONTANAR. Ctra. Granja del Estado.
PISCINA DEL HOTEL CORDOBA-MELIA. Paseo de la Victoria.
PISCINA DEL FRENTE DE JUVENTUDES. Calle Marbella (sector sur).
PISCINA ZARCO. Zarco, 18.
PISCINA PARQUE. Huerta del Sordillo.
PISCINA LA CONCHA. Huerta del Sordillo.
ESTADIO MUNICIPAL EL ARCANGEL.
ESTADIO SAN EULOGIO.
ESTADIO DE LA ELECTROMECANICA.
CAMPOS DE DEPORTE DE LA FEDERACION ANDALUZA DE FUTBOL.
GIMNASIO POLIDEPORTIVO DEL FRENTE DE JUVENTUDES.

CONSULADOS
CONSULATS
CONSULATES
KONSULATE

COLOMBIA. Avda. del Generalísimo, 20. Telf. 22 24 48.
FRANCIA. Aixa, 6. Telf. 23 29 19.
MONACO. Málaga, 6. Telf. 22 43 91.

PORTUGAL. Avda. del Brillante, 161. Telf. 22 19 71 (406).
SUECIA. Carbonell y Morand, 12. Telf. 221120.

BANCOS
BANQUES
BANKS
BANKEN

BANCO DE ESPAÑA. Gran Capitán, 7.
BANCO DE BILBAO. Gran Capitán, 2.
BANCO CENTRAL. Gran Capitán, 12.
BANCO EXTERIOR DE CREDITO. Gran Capitán, 18.
BANCO EXTERIOR DE ESPAÑA. Avda. del Generalísimo, 5.
BANCO HISPANO AMERICANO. Sevilla, 4 y 6.
BANCO IBERICO. Plaza de José Antonio, 5.
BANCO MERIDIONAL. Avda. del Generalísimo, 16.
BANCO DE ANDALUCIA. Cruz Conde, 17.
BANCO RURAL Y MEDITERRANEO. Gondomar, 12.
BANCO DE SANTANDER. Gondomar, 3.
BANCO DE VIZCAYA. Gran Capitán, 4.
CAJA PROVINCIAL DE AHORROS. Gran Capitán, 11.
MONTE DE PIEDAD Y CAJA DE AHORROS DE CORDOBA. Avda. del Generalísimo, 22.

BIBLIOTECAS
BIBLIOTHÈQUES
LIBRAIRES
BIBLIOTHEKEN

BIBLIOTECA PROVINCIAL. Calvo Sotelo. Telf. 22 55 18.
BIBLIOTECA Y HEMEROTECA MUNICIPAL. Sánchez de Feria.
BIBLIOTECA DEL CABILDO CATEDRAL (Para investigadores).
BIBLIOTECA DEL PALACIO EPISCOPAL (Para investigadores).
ARCHIVO HISTORICO PROVINCIAL. Calle de la Encarnación.

SALAS DE EXPOSICION
SALLES DE EXPOSITIONS
EXHIBITION ROOMS
AUSSTELLUNGSSAAL

GALERIA CESPEDES. Círculo de la Amistad. Alfonso XIII, 14. Telf. 22 13 19.
GALERIA LICEO. Círculo de la Amistad. Alfonso XIII, 14. Telf. 22 13 19.
SALA MUNICIPAL DE ARTE. Calle Góngora.
GALERIA DE ARTE ALTAMIRA. Conde de Torres Cabrera, 9. Telf. 22 51 22.
EXPOSICION PERMANENTE DE PRODUCTOS INDUSTRIALES Y ARTESANIA CORDOBESA. Cámara Oficial de Comercio e Industria. Pérez de Castro, 7. Telf. 22 62 76.

PARQUE ZOOLOGICO «JUAN BARASONA».
Parque de Cruz Conde. Telf. 23 31 99.

CUEROS REPUJADOS
CUIRS REPOUSSAGES
EMBOSSED LEATHER
GETRIEBENES LEDER

HIJOS DE DON RAFAEL BERNIER. Encarnación, 8. Telf. 22 22 86.
MERYAN. DON ANGEL LOPEZ OBRERO E HIJOS. Calleja de las Flores, 2. Telf. 22 59 02.
DON JOSE FERNANDEZ MARQUEZ. Villaflor (Calasancio). Telf. 22 62 40.
DON JUAN MARTINEZ CERRILLO. Plaza de San Rafael. Telf. 25 26 94.
EL ZOCO. Calle Judíos.

PLATERIA Y ORFEBRERIA
ORFÉVRERIE
SILVER AND GOLD WORK
SILBER-UND GOLDSCHMIEDEKUNST

HIJOS DE DON MANUEL FRAGERO. Avda. del Generalísimo, 18. Telf. 22 24 06.
DON JOSE GONZALEZ DEL CAMPO. Plaza de San Andrés, 50. Telf. 22 34 04.
DON FRANCISCO RUIZ RUIZ. Enmedio, 13. Telf. 22 23 50.
GONZALEZ ESPELIU, S.R.C. Crucifijos, 6. Telf. 25 17 93.
DON JOSE AGUILAR DE DIOS. Rey Heredia, 29. Telf. 22 39 56.
EL ZOCO. Calle Judíos.

ANTICUARIOS
ANTIQUAIRES
ANTIQUES
ANTIQUITÄTENHÄNDLER

LIBRERIA ANTICUARIA. Diario de Córdoba, 4. Telf. 22 75 69.
DON JUAN RODRIGUEZ MORA. Magistral González Francés, 13. Telf. 22 14 11.
DON JUAN AGUILERA CAÑETE. Encarnación, 7. Telf. 22 32 19.
DON PEDRO PRESA GARCIA (Joyería). San Fernando, 131. Telf. 22 32 27.
DON ANTONIO ADARVE. Torrijos, 6. Telf. 22 42 74.
DON MANUEL VALENZUELA PLANTON (Libros antiguos). Gutiérrez de los Ríos. Telf. 25 36 28.

CAZA Y PESCA

CAZA. Por las condiciones naturales de la provincia la mayor parte de ésta es apta para la caza de perdices, conejos, liebres, palomas, codornices y tórtolas.
En la zona de Hornachuelos-Villaviciosa existen cotos mundialmente famosos de caza mayor, sobre todo en las especies de ciervo y jabalí. También son importantes los cotos de Adamuz y Cardeña.
PESCA. Los principales ríos para la práctica de este deporte son: Retortillo, Bembézar, Guadiato, San Pedro, Guadalmez, Zújar, Arenoso, Arenosillo, Cabra y Guadalquivir.

CHASSE ET PECHE

CHASSE. Etant donné les conditions naturelles de la province, la plus grande partie en est propice à la chasse aux perdrix, aux lapins, aux lièvres, aux pigeons, aux cailles et aux tourterelles.
Dans la région de Hornachuelos-Villaviciosa, il y a des chasses gardées mondialement connues de gros gibier, surtout pour les espèces de cerf et de sanglier. Sont également importantes les chasses gardées d'Adamuz et de Cardeña.
PECHE. Les principales rivières pour la pratique de ce sport sont: le Retortillo, le Bembézar, le Guadiato; le San Pedro, le Guadalmez, le Zújar, l'Arenoso, l'Arenosillo, le Cabra, et le Guadalquivir.

HUNTING AND FISHING

HUNTING. Most of the province is ideal for shooting partridge, rabbit, hare, pigeon, quail and turtle doves.
In the Hornachuelos-Villaviciosa area, there are the world famous big game preserves especially for the hunting of deer and wild boar. The Adamuz and Cardeña game preserves are also important.
FISHING. The main fishing rivers are the Retortillo, Bembézar, Guadiato, San Pedro, Guadalmez, Zújar, Arenoso, Arenosillo, Cabra and Guadalquivir.

JAGD UND FISCHFANG

JAGD. Aufgrund ihrer natürlichen Gegebenheiten ist ein großer Teil der Provinz für die Jagd auf Rebhühner, Hasen, Kaninchen, Tauben, Wachteln und Turteltauben geeignet. In der Gegend von Hornachuelos-Villaviciosa gibt es weltberühmte Jagdreviere für Großwild, vor allem Rotwild und Wildschweine. Auch die Reviere von Adamuz und Cardeña sind bedeutend.
FISCHFANG. Die wichtigsten Flüsse für diesen Sport sind der Retortillo, Bembézar, Guadiato, San Pedro, Guadalmez, Zújar, Arenoso, Arenosillo, Cabra und der Guadalquivir.

EXCURSIONES DESDE CORDOBA A LA PROVINCIA

AGUILAR DE LA FRONTERA. Cabeza de partido judicial, al sur de la provincia. Población superior a los 15.000 habitantes. Son muy interesantes las parroquias de Santa María de Soterraño y de Ntra. Sra. del Carmen, el convento de las Carmelitas Descalzas y la iglesia de la Vera Cruz. La plaza de San José, de forma octogonal, es de singular belleza.

ALMODOVAR DEL RIO. Población de unos 8.000 habitantes. Situado a la orilla derecha del Guadalquivir. Su castillo se encuentra muy bien conservado, presentando gran interés su plaza de armas y sus torres del Moro, la Cuadrada, la Redonda y la Escucha.

BAENA. Cabeza de partido judicial. Población superior a 20.000 habitantes. Principalmente comunicado por la N. 432, Badajoz-Granada, al sur de la provincia. De sus antiguas murallas se conserva la Torre del Sol. Son interesantes la iglesia de Ntra. Sra. de Guadalupe, la Casa del Antiguo Ayuntamiento, la parroquia de Sta. María la Mayor y el convento de San Francisco. Merece especial mención su celebración de la Semana Santa.

CABRA. Cabeza de partido judicial, con más de 20.000 habitantes. Situada al sur, en la zona de campiña. Bien comunicada y próxima a la N-331. Interesante castillo. La iglesia de San Juan Bautista es uno de los templos más antiguos de Andalucía, presentando actualmente, por sus modificaciones aspecto barroco. Muy interesante su parroquia de Ntra. Sra. de la Asunción y Angeles. La Fuente del Río, único manantial vauclasiano de la provincia, ha merecido la calificación de paraje pintoresco. El picacho de la Virgen, con 1.200 metros de altura y donde se encuentra el santuario de la Virgen de la Sierra, por su gran belleza y el paisaje que domina, ha sido declarado Sitio Natural de Interés Nacional.

FUENTE OBEJUNA. Cabeza de partido judicial. Tiene unos 15.000 habitantes. Principalmente comunicada por la N-432, al norte de la provincia. En 1430 logró real privilegio de excepción, siendo dada a D. Pedro Téllez de Girón, gran Maestre de Calatrava. Más tarde, la Orden de Calatrava nombró Gobernador a Don Fernando Gómez de Guzmán, Comendador Mayor de dicha Orden. Los abusos de éste motivaron que el Consejo de la Villa y sus vecinos acordaran darle muerte el 23 de abril de 1.476, hecho que inspiró a Lope de Vega para escribir su inmortal obra. Conjunto urbano de gran tipismo y sabor medieval.

LUCENA. Cabeza de partido judicial. Población superior a 28.000 habitantes. Situada en la campiña, al sur de la provincia. De su primitivo castillo conserva la Torre

del Moral, prisión de Boabdil, que está declarada Monumento Nacional. Interesantes iglesias con valiosas obras de arte, destacando entre ellas la parroquia de San Mateo, cuya capilla del Sagrario es considerada como una joya del barroco. Tiene fama su tradicional industria de velones.

LUQUE. Su población es de 6.700 habitantes. Próxima a la N-432, Badajoz-Granada. Situada en lo alto de un cerro, sobre el que se eleva el castillo. Además del castillo, es muy interesante la iglesia parroquial de Ntra. Sra. de la Asunción, cuyo retablo del altar mayor constituye un excelente muestra del barroco cordobés.

MONTEMAYOR. Población de unos 4.000 habitantes. Situada junto a la N-331. Su castillo se conserva en excelente estado, siendo un curioso ejemplar de construcción militar del siglo XIV, compuesto por tres torres unidas por sólido muro, que enmarcan su plaza de armas. Posee un riquísimo archivo de la Casa Ducal de Frías. También es de interés la parroquia de Ntra. Sra. de la Asunción.

MONTILLA. Cabeza de partido judicial. Población de unos 24.000 habitantes. Situada en la campiña, al sur de la provincia. Muy famosa por la calidad de sus vinos. Interesantes iglesias, conventos y construcciones civiles. Entre sus casas solariegas sobresale la que fue del Inca Garcilaso, hoy Archivo de Protocolos y Municipal, además de Biblioteca Pública. Importantes fiestas de la Vendimia.

MONTORO. Cabeza de partido judicial, con unos 15.000 habitantes. Construida sobre un monte rocoso, rodeado por el Guadalquivir. Próxima a la N-IV. Calles de gran tipismo. Interesantes iglesias y otras construcciones.

MONTURQUE. Población de unos 2.500 habitantes, al sur de Córdoba. De su castillo se conserva una torre y varios lienzos de muralla. Son realmente importantes los silos o aljibes que conserva de su época romana, compuestos de ocho grandes cámaras subterráneas, comunicada entre sí por diversas galerías. Es de interés la parroquia de San Mateo.

PALMA DEL RIO. Su número de habitantes se aproxima a 20.000. Situada en la confluencia del Genil con el Guadalquivir. Pueblo antiquísimo, netamente andaluz, con calles y rincones típicos. Se conservan restos de sus murallas. Interesantes iglesias y conventos, entre los que destaca la parroquia de Ntra. Sra. de la Asunción.

PRIEGO DE CORDOBA. Cabeza de partido judicial. Su población sobrepasa los 25.000 habitantes. Se encuentra al sur de la provincia, en la sierra de su nombre. A unos 18 Km. de la N-432, Badajoz-Granada. Atractivo conjunto urbano. Singular tipismo de la «villa», antiguo barrio hispano-musulmán, cuya estructura se conserva desde el siglo XV con escasas alteraciones. Castillo declarado Monumento Histórico-Artístico. Iglesias interesantes, en las que predomina el barroco. La capilla del Sagrario y el altar mayor de la parroquia de Santa María de la Asunción, el último de estilo plateresco, han sido declarados Monumentos Nacionales. Bellos paseos, plazas y fuentes, entre los que destaca El Adarve, importante balcón desde el que se dominan bellos paisajes, y la Fuente del Rey. Casas señoriales. Celebran en agosto Festivales de España.

PUENTE GENIL. Población de unos 30.000 habitantes, al sur de la provincia. Destaca por su interés y singularidad la celebración de la Semana Santa. Es muy conocida su excelente producción de aceite, vino y carne de membrillo.

ZUHEROS. Tiene unos 2.000 habitantes y se encuentra al sur de Córdoba a cinco kilómetros de la N-432, Badajoz-Granada. Llama poderosamente la atención su situación entre montañas. Su castillo se halla en ruinas. A corta distancia está la «Cueva de los Murciélagos», en la que han aparecido restos humanos del neolítico y diversas piezas de cerámica.

EXCURSIONS A PARTIR DE CORDOUE DANS LA PROVINCE

AGUILAR DE LA FRONTERA. Chef-lieu judiciaire, au sud de la province. Ville de plus de 15.000 habitants. Présentent un intérêt les paroisses de Santa María de Soterraño et de Notre Dame du Carmen, le couvent des Carmelitas Descalzas, et l'église de la Vera Cruz. La place de San José, de forme octogonale, a une singulière beauté.

ALMODOVAR DEL RIO. Ville de quelques 8.000 habitants. Située sur la rive droite du Guadalquivir. Son château est très bien conservé, et ont un grand intérêt sa place d'armes et ses tours du Maure, la tour Cuadrada (Carrée), la Redonda (Ronde) et la Escucha.

BAENA. Chef-lieu judiciaire, ville de plus de 20.000 habitants. Principalement reliée par la N-432, Badajoz-Grenade, au sud de la province. De ses antiques murailles on conserve la Tour du Soleil. Sont intéressants l'église de Notre Dame de Guadalupe, la Maison de l'Ancien Hôtel de Ville, la paroisse de Santa María la Mayor et le couvent de San Francisco. La célébration de la Semaine Sainte y mérite une mention particulière.

CABRA. Chef-lieu judiciaire, de plus de 20.000 habitants. Située au sud, dans la région de campagne. Bien reliée et proche de la N-331. Château intéressant. L'église de San Juan Bautista est l'une des plus anciennes d'Andalousie, et présente actue-

llement, à la suite de modifications, une allure baroque. Sa paroisse de Notre Dame de la Asunción y Angeles est très intéressante. La Fuente del Rio, unique source vauclusienne de la province, a mérité la qualification de coin pittoresque. Le pic de la Vierge, de 1.200 mètres d'altitude et où se trouve le sanctuaire de la Vierge de la Montagne, vu sa grande beauté et le paysage qu'eil domine, a été déclaré Lieu Naturel d'Intérêt National.

FUENTE OBEJUNA. Chef-lieu judiciare, C'est une ville de quelques 15.000 habitants. Principalement reliée par la N-432, au nord de la province. En 1430, elle obtint in privilège royal d'exception, et fut donnée à Pedro Téllez de Girón, Grand Maître de l'ordre de Calatrava. Plus tard l'Ordre de Calatrava nomma comme gouverneur Fernando Gómez de Guzmán, Grand Commandeur de cet Ordre. Ses abus provoquèrent la décision du Conseil de la Ville et de ses habitants de le mettre à mort le 23 avril 1476, ce qui a inspiré la composition de l'immortelle oeuvre de Lope de Vega. Ensemble urbain très typique et d'un grand cachet médiéval.

LUCENA. Chef-lieu judiciare. Ville de plus de 20.000 habitants. Située dans la campagne, au sud de la province. De son château primitif, on conserve la Tour del Moral, prison de Boabdil, qui est déclarée monument national. Intéressantes églises avec de précieuses oeuvres d'art, dont la principale est celle de la paroisse de San Mateo, dont la chapelle du Tabernacle est considérée comme un des joyaux du baroque. Sa traditionnelle industrie de lampes à huile est réputée.

LUQUE. Sa population est de 8.000 habitants. Proche de la N-432, Badajoz-Grenade. Située en haut d'une colline, sur laquelle s'élève le château. En plus du château, est très intéressante l'église paroissiale de Notre Dame de la Asunción, dont le rétable du grand autel constitue un exemple excellent du baroque cordouan.

MONTEMAYOR. Ville de quelques 4.000 habitants. Située à côté de la N-331. Son château est conservé dans un excellent état, et constitue un exemplaire curieux de la construction militaire du XIVème siècle, composé de trois tours unies par une solide muraille, qui limitent sa place d'armes. Elle possède des Archives très riches de la Maison Ducale de Frías. Est également intéressante la paroisse de Notre Dame de la Asunción.

MONTILLA. Chef-lieu judiciaire. Population de quelques 24.000 habitants. Située dans la campagne, au sud de la province. Très célèbre par la qualité de ses vins. Eglises, couvents et constructions civiles intéressants. Parmi ses Manoirs se détache celle de l'Inca Garcilaso, aujourd'hui Archives de

179

Protocole et Municipales, en plus d'être Bibliothèque Publique. Importantes fêtes de la vendange.

MONTORO. Chef-lieu juridique, de quelques 15.000 habitants. Construite sur une montagne rocheuse, entourée par le Guadalquivir. Proche de la N-IV. Rues très typiques. Eglises et autres constructions intéressantes.

MONTURQUE. Ville de quelques 2.500 habitants, au sud de Cordoue. De son château on conserve une tour et plusieurs pans de muraille. Sont réellement importants les silos ou citernes qu'elle conserve de l'époque romaine, composés de huit grandes chambres souterraines reliées entre elles par diverses galeries. La paroisse de San Mateo est intéressante.

PALMA DEL RIO. Le nombre de ses habitants est de près de 20.000. Située au confluent du Genil et du Guadalquivir. Ville très ancienne, nettement andalouse, avec des rues et des coins typiques. On conserve des restes de ses murailles. Eglises et couvents intéressants, parmi lesquels se distingue la paroisse de Notre Dame de la Asunción.

PRIEGO DE CORDOBA. Chef-lieu judiciaire. Sa population dépasse les 20.000 habitants. Elle se trouve au sud de la province, dans la sierra du même nom. A quelques 18 Km. de la N-432, Badajoz-Grenade. Bel ensemble urbain. La «Villa», ancien quartier hispano-musulmán singulièrement typique, dont la structure se conserve depuis le XVème siècle avec très peu de changements. Château déclaré Monument Historique Artistique. Eglises intéressantes, dans lesquels prédomine le baroque. La chapelle du Tabernacle et le grand autel de la paroisse de Santa María de la Asunción, ce dernier de style plateresque, ont été déclarés Monuments Nationaux. Belles promenades, places et fontaines, parmi lesquels se distinguent l'Adarve, important balcon d'où on domine de beaux paysages, et la Fuente del Rey. Maisons seigneuriales. En août se célèbrent les Festivals d'Espagne.

PUENTE GENIL. Ville de quelques 30.000 habitants, au sud de la province. S'y distingue pour son intérêt et sa singularité la célébration de la Semaine Sainte. Son excellente production d'huile, de vin et de gelée de coings est très connue.

ZUHEROS. Elle a quelques 2.000 habitants et se trouve au sud de la province de Cordoue à cinq kilomètres de la N-432, Badajoz-Grenade. Sa situation entre les montagnes qui l'entourent, à 660 mètres, rappelle puissamment le regard. Son château est en ruines. A peu de distance se trouve la «Caverne des Chauves-Souris», où sont apparus des restes humains du néolithique et différentes pièces de céramique.

EXCURSIONS FROM CORDOBA AROUND THE PROVINCE

AGUILAR DE LA FRONTERA. Seat of jurisdictional district in the south of the province. It has over 15,000 inhabitants. The parish churches of Santa María de Soterraño and of Our Lady of Carmen are very interesting, also the Convent of the Barefoot Carmelites and the Vera Cruz church. The octagonal St. Joseph Square is singularly beautiful.

ALMODOVAR DEL RIO. Has about 8,000 inhabitants and lies on the right bank of the Guadalquivir River. Its castle has been kept in very good condition and its square of arms and the towers: the Moor's Tower, the Square Tower, the Round Tower and the Listening Tower, are extremely interesting.

BAENA. Seat of jurisdictional district. It has over 20,000 inhabitants. Its main means of communication is by the Badajoz-Granada road, the N-432, to the south of the province. Of the old ramparts, the Sun Tower has been preserved. The church of Our Lady of Guadalupe, the façade of the ancient Town Hall, the parish church of Santa María la Mayor and the San Francisco convent. The Easter Week celebration are worthy of being specially mentioned.

CABRA. Seat of jurisdictional district. It has over 20,000 inhabitants and lies to the south in the flat arable area. It is very well communicated and is near the N-331 road. The castle is of great interest and the St. John the Baptist church is one of the oldest in Andalucía, although the changes made give it a barroque look. The parish church of Our Lady of the Assumption and the Angels is also of interest. The fresh water spring, the Fuente del Río, hasearned the fame of being a very pictoresque landscape. The peak of the Virgen, 1,200 metres high where the the shrine of the Virgen de la Sierra is to be found, has been called Natural Spot of National Interest because of its beauty and the views it commands.

FUENTE OBEJUNA. Seat of jurisdictional distric. It has about 15,000 inhabitants and its main means of communication is by the N-432 road to the north of the province. In 1430 it was given to D. Pedro Téllez de Girón, Grand Master of Calatrava, thus obtaining royal privilege of exception. Later on, the Order of Calatrava appointed Don Fernando Gómez de Guzmán, Chief Commander of the Order, as Governor, but the abuse made of this appointment caused his death by the Council of the Villa on 23rd April, 1476. This inspired Lope, de Vega to write his immortal masterpiece. The town on the whole is typical and still retains its mediaeval savour.

LUCENA. Seat of jurisdictional district. It has over 28,000 inhabitants and lies in the flat arable area to the south of the province. Of its original castle, the Boabdil prison, the Tower of Moral, which has been declared a National Monument. There are interesting churches with several religious works of art, among which the parish church of St. Matthew stands out, and the chapel of the Sacrarium is considered to be an excellent example of Baroque art. The tradition industry of brass lamps is famed.

LUQUE. It has 6,700 inhabitants and is near the Badajoz-Granada road, the N-432. It stands on the ridge of a hill and over it rises the castle. Besides the castle, the parish church of Our Lady of the Assumption is of extreme interest. The altar piece on the high altar is an excellent example of Cordovan Baroque art.

MONTEMAYOR. It has about 4,000 inhabitants and is near the N-331 road. The castle, which is still in very good condition, is a strange example of military building during the 14th century. It is made up of three towers joined together by solid walls which enclose its arms square. The archives in the Ducal House of Frías are rich in quantity and variety. The parish church of Our Lady of the Assumption is also very interesting.

MONTILLA. Seat of jurisdictional district. It has about 24,000 inhabitants and lies in the flat arable area to the south of the province. It is reknowned for the quality of its wines. Its churches, convents and lay buildings are all of interst. Of the houses belonging to ancient and noble families, Inca Garcilaso's, now the Municipal and Protocol Archive, as well as the Public Library is the most excellent example. Important «fiestas» are held during the grape harvesting season.

MONTORO. Seat of jurisdictional district. It is built on a rocky hill and the Guadalquivir River flows round it. It is near the N-IV road. The streets are very typical and the churches and other buildings are interesting.

MONTURQUE. It has about 2,500 inhabitants and lies to the south of Córdoba. A tower and several stretches of the rampart of the castle still stand. The silos and wells preserved from Roman times are of great importance. They are made of eight large underground chambers communicated by several passages. The St. Matthew parish church is interesting.

PALMA DEL RIO. Its inhabitants number about 20,000 and it lies in the confluence of the Genil River and the Guadalquivir River. It is an extremely ancient village which is typically Andalucian with its streets and corners. The remains of the ramparts have been preserved. The churches and convents are all interesting, especially the parish church of Our Lady of the Assumption.

PRIEGO DE CORDOBA. Seat of jurisdictional district. It has over 25,000 inhabitants and lies to the south of the province, in the mountain ranges of the same name. It is about 18 Km. from the Badajoz-Granada road, the N-432. It is on the whole an attractive town with a very typical «villa», the old Spanish-Moslem quarter, the structure of which has been preserved since the 15th century with very few changes. The castle has been declared a Historical and Artistic Monument. The churches, in which the Baroque style predominantes, are very interesting. The Sacrarium Chapel and the high altar in the parish church of St. Mary of the Assumption, the last church to be built in the 16th century Spanish style using silver ornamentation, have been declared National Monuments. It has beautiful walks, squares and fountains, the most outstanding of which is the Adarve, important balcony from where views of beautiful landscapes are commanded, and the Fuente del Rey. The manor houses should also be included. The Festivals of Spain are celebrated here in August.

PUENTE GENIL. It has over 30,000 inhabitants and lies to the south of the province. It stands out for its interesting and extraordinary Easter Week celebrations. Famed for its production of excellent olive oil, wine and quince jam.

ZUHEROS. It has 2,000 inhabitants and lies to the south of Córdoba, about 5 Km. from the Badajoz-Granada road, the N-432. It is surrounded by mountains of 660 metres, which makes it noteworthy. Its castle is in ruins. Nearby, is the Cave of the Bats, where Neolithic human remains have been found and several pieces of pottery.

AUSFLÜGE IN DIE PROVINZ VON CORDOBA

AGUILAR DE LA FRONTERA. Hauptstadt eines Gerichtsbezirks, in Süden der Provinz. Mehr als 15.000 Einwohner. Sehr interessant sind die Pfarreikirchen von Santa Maria de Soterraño und Ntra. Señora del Carmen, das Kloster der Barfüßigen Karmeliterinnen, und die Kirche de la Vera Cruz. Die achteckige Plaza San José ist von einzigartiger Schönheit.

ALMODOVAR DEL RIO. Etwa 8.000 Einwohner. Am rechten Ufer des Guadalquivir gelegen. Das schloß ist sehr gut erhalten. Von großem Interesse sind sein Exerzierplatz und die vier Türme— del Moro, la Cuadrada, la Redonda und la Escucha.

BAENA. Hauptstadt eines Gerichtsbezirks.

Mehr als 20.000 Einwohner. Liegt an der N. 432 Badajoz-Granada, im Süden der Provinz. Von den alten Stadtmauern ist noch der Torre del Sol erhalten. Von Bedeutung sind die Kirche de Nuestra Señora de Guadalupe, das alte Ratshaus, die Pfarrkirche Sta. María la Mayor und das Kloster San Francisco. Besonders erwähnenswert ist die Prozession der Karwoche.

CABRA. Hauptstadt eines Gerichtsbezirks, mit mehr als 20.000 Einwohnern. Liegt im Südlichen Flachland. Mit guten Verkehrsverbindungen, nahe der N-331. Bedeutendes schloß. Die Kirche San Juan Bautista ist eine der ältesten Andalusiens die jetzt aufgrund Renovierungen Barrockzüge aufweist. Von großen Interesse die Pfarreikirche von Ntra. Señora de la Asunción y Angeles. Der Fuente del Rio, der einzige vauklasianische Quellfluß der Provinz, verdient es, als maierisch Ort bezeichnet zu werden. Der Berggipfel Unseser iieben Frau, mit einer Höhe von 1.200 m, auf dem sich die Kapelle der Virgen de la Sierra befindet, wurde seiner großen Schönheit und der ihn umgebenden Landschaft wiiien zum Naturschutzgebiet erkiärt.

FUENTE OBEJUNA. Hauptstadt eines Gerichtsbezirks. Ungefähr 15.000 Einwohner. Hauptverkehrsverbindung die N-432 im Norden der Provinz. 1430 erhielt sie das Königliche Ausnahmeprivileg und wurde an Pedro Téllez de Girón, Großmeister des Ordens von Calatrava, vergeben. Später wurde Fernando Gómez de Guzmán, Grokomtur des Ordens, zum Gouverneur ernannt. Der Stadtrat und die Bürger beschlossen am 23. April 1476, ihn wegen Mißbrauchs seiner Gewalt zu töten. Dies inspirierte Lope de Vega zu seinem unsterblichen Werk. Gemeinde mit großen Lokaikoiorit und mittelalterlichen Reminiszenzen.

LUCENA. Hauptstadt eines Gerichtsbezirks. Mehr als 28.000 Einwohner. Im südlichen Flachland der Provinz. Von seiner aiten Burg ist der Torre del Moral erhaiten, einst Gefängnis Boabdils, das unter Denkmaisschutz gestellt wurde. Kirchen von großem Interesse mit wertvollen Kunstwerken, unter anderen die Pfarrkirche San Mateo, deren Capilla del Sagrario als ein Juwel des Barrocks gilt. Die traditionelle Öllampenindustrie ist berühmt.

LUQUE. 6.700 Einwohner. Nähe der N-432 Badajoz-Granada. Liegt auf einem Hügel, der von der Burg gekrönt wird. Neben der Burg ist auch die Pfarreikirche von Ntra. Sra. de la Asunción von großem Interesse, deren Altarblatt ein ausgezeichnetes Beispiel des kordobesischen Barrocks darstellt.

MONTEMAYOR. Etwa 4.000 Einwohner. Liegt in der Nähe der N-331. Seine Burg, ein seltsames militärisches Bauwerk des 14. Jahrhunderts, ist sehr gut erhalten. Es besteht aus drei Türnen, die von einer kräftigen Mauer verbunden werden, die den Exerzierplatz umgiet. Ebenfalls von Interesse ist die Pfarreikirche Ntra. Sra. de la Asunción.

MONTILLA. Hauptstadt eines Gerichtsbezirks. Etwa 24.000 Einwonner. Liegt im südlichen Flachland der Provinz. Sehr berühmt seines Weines wegen. Kirchen, Klöster und sekuläre Bauwerke von Interesse. Unter seinen Herrenhäusern sticht hervor das des Inkas Garcilaso, heute Städtisches Archiv und Stadtbibliothek. Wichtige Weinfeste.

MONTORO. Hauptstadt eines Gerichtsbezirks mit 15.000 Einwohnern. Auf einem felsigen Berg erbaut, umgeben vom Guadalquivir. Nähe der N-IV. Straßen mit viel Lokalkolorit. Kirchen von großen Interesse und andere Bauwerke.

MONTURQUE. Etwa 2.500 Einwohner, im Süden Córdobas. Von seinem Burg sind ein Turm und etliche Mauerreste erhalten. Wirklich bedeutend sind die Getreidespeicher oder Zisternen aus derrömischen Zeit, die aus acht großen, durch verschiedene Gänge miteinander verbundenen, unterirdischen Kammern bestehen. Von Interesse ist auch die Pfarreikirche von San Mateo.

PALMA DEL RIO. Annähernd 20.000 Einwohner. Liegt an Zusammenfluß des Genil mit dem Guadalquivir. Eine uralte typisch andalusische Siedlung mit ihren Straßen und Winkeln. Es sind noch Mauernreste erhalten. Interessante Kirchen und Klöster; besonders hervorstehend die Pfarreikirche von Ntra. Sra. de la Asunción.

PRIEGO DE CORDOBA. Hauptstadt eines Gerichtsbezirks. Mehr als 25.000 Einwohner. Befindet sich im Süden der Provinz, in der Sierra gleichen Namens. Ungefähr 18 km von der N-432 Badajoz-Granada entfernt. Reizvolle Stadt. Einzigartiges Lokalkolorit der alten «villa» dem spanisch-musulmanischen Stadtteil, dessen Struktur seit dem 15. Jahrhundert mit wenigen Änderungen erhalten blieb. Die Burg steht unter Denkmalschutz. Kirchen, vor allem barrocke, von großem Interesse. Die Kapelle des Allerheiligsten und der Hochaltar der Pfarreikirche Sta. María de la Asunción, der letzte im platereskem Stil entstandene, wurden unter Denkmalschutz gestellt. Schöne Spazierwege, Plätze und Brunnen, unter denen El Adarve, von dem aus man die schöne Landschaft überblickt, hervorsticht, und la Fuente del Rey. Herrenhäuser. Im August werden die Festivales de España gefeiert.

PUENTE GENIL. Etwa 30.000 Einwohner, im Süden der Provinz. Einzigartiges Begehen der Karwoche. Bekannt für die ausgezeichnete Herstellung von Wein, Öl, und Quittengelee.

ZUHEROS. Etwa 2.000 Einwohner und liegt im Süden Córdobas, 5 km von der N-432

Badajoz-Granada. Aufsehenerregende Lage im Gebirge. Die Burg ist in Ruinen. Nicht weit entfernt davon findet sich die «Höhle der Fledermause» (Cueva de los murciélagos), wo man menschlishe Reste und Keramika aus dem Neolithischen Zeitalter fand.

DISTANCIAS KILOMÉTRICAS DESDE CORDOBA Á:

DISTANCES KILOMETRIQUES DEPUIS CORDOBA A:

DISTANCE IN KILOMETERS FROM CORDOBA TO:

ENTFERNUNGEN IN KM. VON CORDOBA NACH:

Baena	61
Hinojosa del Duque	98
Pozoblanco	73
Fuente Obejuna	92
Montoro	41
Bujalance	39
Posadas	36
La Rambla	45

Aguilar	55
Montilla	48
Cabra	76
Priego de Córdoba	107
Rute	100
Lucena	75
Castro del Río	42
Zuheros	71
Puente Genil	73
Palma del Río	67
Monturque	65
Montemayor	39
Luque	70
Almodóvar del Río	32

* * *

Ciudad Real	198
Badajoz	272
Sevilla	138
Málaga	187
Granada	166
Jaén	104
Madrid	403
Barcelona	880
Coruña	1.006

INDICE